ON THE EDGE OF A COUNTRY
Memoir of a young girl under Nazi fascism

"With the present day rise of anti-semitism in Europe it is important seventy years after the Holocaust to make Europeans aware that Jews were not the only victims of Hitler. Slavic people, such as the Slovenes, political opponents of the Nazis, the handicapped, the Church, Gypsies, homosexuals and many other groups were singled out for persecution.

Milena's dramatic story reveals the struggle of her family of eleven, each in his own way, to fight first the Italians, and then the Germans, some in the resistance, others by surviving the death camps. A timely story."

> — Ina R. Friedman, author of *The Other Victims: First Person Stories of Non-Jews Persecuted by the Nazis* (Houghton Mifflin)

"One cannot truly begin to imagine the horrors of the time . . . but walk in the shoes of a girl named Milena and you will get a clearer idea of what she, her brave family and her oppressed people were forced to endure. Hollenbaugh's lovingly-told story adds pertinence and meaning to the historical events of a very dark time in history. A well-researched and thought-provoking work, this story serves the important service of filling the gaps in our understanding of the time; it is a significant gift to this and future generations."

> — Mary Beth Egeling
> Author of *Tell Me What You CAN Do*

ON THE EDGE OF A COUNTRY

To Brian and Chris—
With much
appreciation and
best wishes.
Silvia
2/16

ON THE EDGE OF A COUNTRY

Memoir of a young girl under
Nazi fascism

Silvia Hollenbaugh

Library of Congress Control Number: 2015904206
ISBN-13: 978-0-9961291-0-7

Published by SZS Books, LLC
szsbooks1@gmail.com

Cover photo: Courtesy of Musei Provinciali, Gorizia
Cover Design: Julie Eggers

Dedicated to my mother,

the memory of my grandfather and uncle,

and to those whose stories can never be told.

CONTENTS

PRONUNCIATION GUIDE

The following Slovenian letters, which I have included to aid in the pronunciation of Slovenian names and places in the book, are pronounced approximately as the bold letters in the following English words:

    c   as in pi**zz**a

    č   as in **ch**ocolate

    j   as in **y**es

    š   as in **ch**ampagne

    ž   as in mea**s**ure

    a   as in **a**lphabet

    e   as in h**ay**

    i   as b**ee**t

    o   as in **o**pen

    u   as in m**oo**n

GLOSSARY

Achtung!: Attention! (German)

Adriatic Littoral: Territory (Austrian Littoral) which Italian irrendentists considered an unredeemed part of their nation and included Gorizia, Trieste and the Istrian Peninsula

Allies in World War I: France, Great Britain, Russia, United States, Japan, Italy, Serbia, Greece, Belgium and more than ten other countries around the world

Allies in World War II: France, Great Britain, Russia, United States, Poland, Greece, Yugoslavia, China, among others

Allied Military Government (AMG): The form of military rule administrated by the Allied forces during and after World War II within European territories they occupied

Axis in World War II: Germany, Italy, Japan, Independent State of Croatia, Bulgaria, Hungary, Romania, Finland, among others

Asilo: Preschool

Bandit (singular) or Banditen (plural): Literally bandit, outlaw; term used to refer to anyone associated with the partisans or the Resistance Movement (German)

(La) Befana: The kind, old witch who brings presents on January 6 for the Epiphany (Italian)

Binkošti: The religious holiday called Pentacost, falling on the seventh Sunday after Easter. Also referred to as White Sunday, from the white garments worn by those baptized on that day (Slovenian)

Blackshirts: Armed squads organized under Mussolini's Fascist Party to terrorize

Bociada: Big mouth (variation of the Friulian word, *bociata*)

Briscola: A card game (Italian)

Brodo: A homemade broth common in this border area, made with beef or chicken, usually with homemade pasta or rice added (Italian)

Camomilla: Chamomile tea (Italian)

Cantina: Cellar, often wine cellar (Italian)

Carabiniere: A member of the Italian national police force, which is a division of the military (Italian)

Centesimo: A coin of the value of one-hundredth of an Italian lira used at that time; centesimi is the plural of centesimo (Italian)

Central Powers in World War I: Germany, Austria-Hungary, Ottoman Empire, Bulgaria

Cresima: Confirmation, as in the Catholic Church (Italian)

Croce Verde: A local, volunteer organization which provided emergency and medical assistance (Italian)

DDT (dichloro diphenyl trichloroethane): Often prepared as a dusting powder to destroy lice; commonly used during typhus epidemics, especially in the concentration camps after World War II

Decima Mas: An independent military corps created in 1943 to provide support for the Germans against the Allies and partisans; infamous for its episodes of criminal violence and torture (Italian)

Famiglia numerosa: Large family (Italian)

Franz Josef: Head of Austrian Habsburg Empire from 1848 until his death in 1916

Italian irredentists: (From Italian *irredento*, or "unredeemed") Italian nationalists who advocated the recovery of territory under a foreign government; in this case, the Adriatic Littoral, which was part of the Austro-Hungarian Empire

Lager: Concentration camp, from Konzentrationslager, or KZ (German)

La penna nera* or *La penna sul cappello: A song of the legendry Alpine Corps, a distinct mountain infantry corps of the Italian Army that fought during WWI. It sings of the black feather on the traditional hat of the Alpine soldier. The Alpine group was famous for its songs and choirs. (Italian)

Lira: (Plural: lire) National currency of Italy until the European Union adopted the euro (Italian)

Kapo: Head of a group of prisoners or of a work detail, often a prisoner of the same ethnic group (German: *Kapo*; Italian: *Kapò*)

Kohlrabi: Turnip cabbage, a type of vegetable common in Germany

Milenka: Nickname of endearment for Milena (Slovene)

Minestra: Vegetable soup (Italian)

Municipio: Municipal building (Italian)

Nona, Nono: The Slovenian terms for grandmother, grandfather used in the border region (from the Italian, *nonna, nonno*)

Obrni ret: Turn your bottom around. (*'Ret'* is dialect for *'rit'* in standard Slovene.)

Osteria: Tavern (Italian)

Omelette: A crepe-like dessert, filled with marmalade, nuts or chocolate (French term used in Italy and Italian-Slovenian border region)

Partisan: A member of an organized civilian force fighting covertly to drive out occupying enemy troops

Pasta e fagioli: A regional Italian soup made with beans and pasta (Italian)

Polenta: A staple food of the region made from corn flour (Italian)

Raus!: Out! (German)

Rastrellamento: The combing of an occupied area by an armed force in order to eliminate suspected enemies or take revenge upon a population, such as the round-ups of civilians captured by fascists and Nazis during their occupation during WWII (Italian)

Revier: Abbreviation for the word, *Krankenrevier*; which means *infirmary*, but within the Bergen-Belsen concentration camp, a place that is more of a death room (German)

Scabbia: Scabies (Italian)

Schnell!: Fast! (German)

SS or Schutzstaffel: The elite military and police unit of the Nazi Party; literally 'protective squadron' (German)

Tabacchino: A small shop that sells tobacco products, as well as other types of small merchandise (Italian)

Tata: Dad or Daddy (Slovene)

Tessera: Card, pass or ticket (Italian)

Tribunale: Courthouse (Italian)

Verfluchte Banditen!: Damn bandits! (German)

Viva il Re, Viva il Duce: Long Live the King, Long Live the Chief. *Duce* was a particular title given to Benito Mussolini. (Italian)

Wehrmacht: The German Armed Forces other than the SS (German)

Present-Day Italy

Friuli-Venezia
Giulia

Udine
Milan
Gorizia
Venice
Trieste

ITALY

Bologna
Florence

ADRIATIC
SEA

Arezzo

Rome

Naples

SARDINIA

SICILY

FRIULI-VENEZIA GIULIA
REGION
WITHIN PRESENT-DAY
ITALY

MILES
0   60

0   100
KILOMETERS
(approximate)

Under the Habsburg Empire

AUSTRO-HUNGARIAN
EMPIRE

ITALY

• Udine

• Gorizia

• Vrtojba

• Ljubljana

Trieste •

ADRIATIC
SEA

ISTRIA

Rijeka •

Pula •

AUSTRO-ITALIAN
BOUNDARY
1866-1918

MILES
0   25

KILOMETERS
0   40
(approximate)

Under Italy after World War I

AUSTRIA

ITALY

KINGDOM of
SERBS, CROATS
& SLOVENES
(YUGOSLAVIA)

Udine

Gorizia

Vertoiba
(Vrtojba)

Ljubljana

Trieste

ADRIATIC
SEA

Fiume
(Rijeka)

ISTRIA

Pola
(Pula)

POST WORLD WAR I
ITALO-YUGOSLAV
BORDER
1924

MILES
0   25

KILOMETERS
0   40
(approximate)

Gorizia Separated from Its Suburbs after WWII

AUSTRIA

ITALY

YUGOSLAVIA

• Udine

• Ljubljana

Gorizia •
Vrtojba

Trieste •

ADRIATIC
SEA

ISTRIA

• Rijeka

• Pula

POST WORLD WAR II
ITALO-YUGOSLAV
BORDER
1954

0   MILES   25

0   KILOMETERS   40
(approximate)

After Slovenian Independence from Yugoslavia

ITALY

SLOVENIA

Tolmin

Mozirje-Smartno
ob Paki
(70 km)

Ljubljana

Lokve

Solkan
Nova Gorica
Gorizia Šempeter
Vrtojba Šempas
Bilje Dornberk
Miren
Renče

Postojna

Grado

Trieste

ADRIATIC
SEA

ISTRIA

CROATIA

ITALO-SLOVENIAN
BORDER
1991-PRESENT DAY

0	MILES	15

0	KILOMETERS	25
(approximate)

HISTORICAL BACKGROUND

This memoir tells the story of a young Slovenian girl named Milena, growing up in Fascist Italy. The background, with accompanying maps, is intended to provide the reader with a basic foundation to understand the historical events that affected the lives of Milena, her family members, as well as many others from the Slovenian minority population in the region of Venezia Giulia within Italy.

Milena's homeland

In the northeastern corner of Italy, with the Adriatic Sea to the south and the snow-capped Julian Alps rising to the north, lies Friuli-Venezia Giulia.[1] Within this region bordered by Austria and Slovenia, Milena lived near the city of Gorizia, which is located on Italy's current northeastern edge.

The Slovenian people began to permanently settle along the Isonzo-Soča River[2] in the sixth to seventh centuries. By the Middle Ages they were considered a distinct, however small, ethnic group. Although the territory on which the Slovenian people have lived has remained relatively the same, political borders have changed. Within the last hundred years, Milena's hometown of Vrtojba, a suburb of Gorizia, has been in four different countries. (See map illustrations.)

World War I and the Austrian Littoral (Map illustration x)

The turbulent political history which affected Milena's life began when World War I ushered in a change of borders for this part of Europe. Since the 1800s, many ethnicities, including the Slovenes and other Slavic populations, had been under the Habsburg rule of the Austro-Hungarian Empire. Rising feelings of nationalism among these groups fueled events that contributed to the outbreak of World War I. As a result, in 1914 the Empire declared war on Serbia, and soon the Central Powers of Austria-Hungary, Germany and the Ottoman Empire were fighting against the Allies (including Britain, France and Russia) that had aligned themselves with Serbia.

Under the Empire, *Küstenland*, also known by the Slovenes as Austrian *Primorje* or the Austrian Littoral, was of great strategic importance. It included Trieste, the prominent seaport on the Adriatic, the province of Gorizia, and the Istrian Peninsula stretching south into the Adriatic Sea. Italian irredentists considered the Austrian Littoral unredeemed Italian territory, so when the Allied forces of France, Britain and Russia promised this land to the Kingdom of Italy under the 1915 Treaty of London, the secret pact persuaded Italy to enter World War I on the side of the Allies.

Dissolution of the Empire—the Austrian Littoral is annexed to Italy (Map illustration xi)

With the military defeat of the Central Powers came the breakup of the Austro-Hungarian Empire, and the land on which these Slovenes had lived together became divided into two separate countries. Part of the Austro-Hungarian territory, which had been mostly inhabited by Slovenes and Croatians, united with other Slavish groups in 1918. This created the Kingdom of Serbs, Croats and Slovenes, which became the Kingdom of Yugoslavia in 1929. As a result of the Allied victory, Italy did indeed gain the approximate geographic boundaries of the Austrian Littoral, which the Italians called the Adriatic Littoral and included what was later referred to as Venezia Giulia. In addition to acquiring this expected territory, Rijeka (Fiume in Italian) was, in 1922, claimed by Italy, extending its borders even farther than the Treaty of London had promised. Consequently, 340,000 Slovenes and 160,000 Croatians (primarily in Istria), who had formerly been ruled under the Austrian Habsburgs, had now become residents of the centralized national state of the Kingdom of Italy.[3]

In 1920, the Treaty of Rapallo between the Kingdom of Italy and the Kingdom of Serbs, Croats and Slovenes settled some disputes over territory from the dissolution of the Austro-Hungarian Empire. It required the Kingdom of Serbs, Croats and Slovenes to be responsible for the minority rights of a population of approximately a few thousand ethnic Italians on its newly acquired territory, but no formal conditions were required of the Kingdom of Italy toward the half-million Slavic residents who now lived in Venezia Giulia.[4] It soon became clear to these Slovenian and Croatian residents of Italy that the relative tolerance of the old Empire would not be equaled by this new nation.

Slavic discrimination and persecution under Fascist Italy

Benito Mussolini founded the first Fascist political group in Italy in 1919. By 1922 the Fascist Party had become so powerful that Italy's King Victor Emmanuel III was forced to recognize him as head of the government. As "Founder of the Empire," Mussolini turned Italy into a totalitarian state and, through his armed squads, the Blackshirts, violence was used to destroy all political opposition. Mussolini had imperialistic goals to restore Italy's glory by extending its territory in the creation of a new Empire.

As this Italian Fascist movement under Dictator Benito Mussolini gained strength, in Venezia Giulia it manifested itself with extreme Slavic discrimination. The derogatory word *s'ciavi*, meaning "slaves," became a common synonym for people of Slavic heritage. Gradually, anti-Slavic persecution was incorporated into the policy of the region. Fascist propaganda "relentlessly tried to demonstrate the superiority of Italian culture."[5] "The Italians escalated their actions by deliberate attempts to undermine the Slovenian minority's economy, which—not unlike the cultural and political life of Slovenes—was frequently more prosperous than most Italian companies and organizations."[6] The use of the Slovenian language in public was prohibited. Slovenian economic,

4

political, and cultural organizations were dissolved. Slovenian newspapers were banned and schools were either closed or the use of their language was prohibited. Slovenian names of people and places were Italianized, and Slovenian inscriptions on gravestones were removed. This *bonifica etnica*, or "ethnic cleansing," was carried out systematically by the Fascist regime from the end of World War I through World War II in order to wipe out all elements of Slovenian language and culture.

One of the first public demonstrations of violence in the region occurred in the nearby port city of Trieste in 1920. Fascist Blackshirts burned down the *Narodni Dom*, the Slavic Cultural Center, which had stood as a symbol that Trieste (*Trst* in Slovene) also had roots as a Slavic city. This took place two years before Mussolini's Fascist regime came to power in 1922. In his book, *Necropolis*, Slovenian Trieste resident Boris Pahor wrote of this evil event from his youth: "The blood-red sky above the harbor, the wild fascists who dumped gasoline on the proud building and then danced around its furious pyre—all this impressed itself on the child's mind, traumatizing it."[7]

Outbreaks of brutality spread to the city and surrounding area of Gorizia, which had a significant Slovenian presence. As early as 1921, Slovenian Archbishop Frančišek Borgija Sedej had written a letter to the Vatican reporting on fascist violence toward this minority consisting of approximately a third of the municipal population.[8] Sedej faced persecution, along with other Slovenian clergy, intellectuals and Slovenian officials in the region.[9]

In 1926, fascists invaded Gorizia's *Trgovski Dom* in an attempt to eradicate the ethnic Slovenian presence entirely. Constructed in 1904, this building was the seat of the Slovenian Commerce and Cultural Association, housed with a theater, music school and library. Musical instruments, furniture, and Slovenian books were hurled from windows and set afire. Fascists occupied the building, renaming it *Casa del Fascio*, or "House of the Fascists."[10]

Lojze Bratuž, a Slovenian choirmaster and composer, is considered one martyr of the anti-fascist struggle. In 1936, he was kidnapped by an Italian fascist squad after attending Mass, beaten and forced to drink a mixture of gasoline and motor oil. Bratuž died two months later in the hospital of Gorizia.[11]

Similar scenes were repeated countless times across the region as fascists tried to remove all traces of Slovenian culture. It was in this little-known part of the world that Milena, made to feel like a second-class citizen, spent her youth.

Response to Slavic persecution

In response to the oppression, about 70,000 Italian Slavs are reported to have emigrated.[12] Slovenes living in Italy crossed the border to Yugoslavia or immigrated to South America or the United States. In the second half of the 1920s, TIGR, the pioneer of anti-fascist resistance movements in Europe, was formed. An acronym for Trieste, Istria, Gorizia and Rijeka, it "responded to fascist violence with violence ... and ... tried to instill courage in the local population ...."[13] "Between the fall of 1929 and the spring of 1930, more than sixty members of the movement were arrested, some were shot, and others sentenced to long prison terms."[14]

Figure 1. Strolling down Corso Verdi, people stop to look at a window display at Trgovski Dom. The building was designed by architect, Max Fabiani.
Courtesy of *Isonzo Soča, Giornale di Frontiera* (Foto: Musei Provinciali, Gorizia)

Slavic persecution in Yugoslavia during the World War II Nazi and Italian occupation

Violence intensified with the advent of World War II, which began with the German attack upon Poland on September 1, 1939. The Axis Powers, which, along with Germany, included Hungary, Romania, Italy and Bulgaria, moved across the continent, devastating and occupying much of Europe.

Mussolini joined Hitler's Germany in June 1940, with the hope of expanding Italian boundaries even farther. By early 1942, most major countries of the world had become involved in a war that would end in 1945 with a new world order.[15]

As World War II progressed, Slavic persecution was felt across borders, when the Slovenes and other Slavic groups in Yugoslavia began to experience the brutality of the Nazis and the Italian fascists. Having been pressured by Nazi Germany to join the Axis Powers, the government of Yugoslavia finally signed the Tripartite Pact with Germany, Italy and Japan. However, the defeat of Yugoslavia's pro-Axis regime by a military coup, along with mass demonstrations in response to the controversial pact, led Hitler to move swiftly to destroy the country of Yugoslavia. Only one week later, on April 6, 1941, Germany launched the attack on the nation. Bulgarians invaded from the east, German forces from the north, and the Italian army from the west. The Yugoslav defense collapsed, and the country was occupied by Nazi Germany and Fascist Italy, along with other Axis forces.[16]

As a result, in the Slovenian and Croatian regions of Yugoslavia which were occupied by Italy, the fascists attempted to destroy all elements which had given these populations a national awareness, as had been done to the Slovenian minority population in Venezia Giulia. Many Slovenian and Croatian civilians were deported to Italian concentration camps. Fascist anti-Slav and anti-communist policy had reached a "culmination in the Italian participation of the invasion and dismemberment of Yugoslavia."[17]

Anti-fascist resistance movements

This violence gave rise to many resistance movements across Yugoslavia, the most successful of which was the partisan group led by Josip Broz Tito and the Communist Party of Yugoslavia. The idea of communism among anti-fascists, including Slovenes in both Italy and Yugoslavia, had become a growing force in the 1930s. "Venezia Giulia had one of Italy's most robust and well-organized communist anti-fascist groups" struggling for social justice and freedom.[18]   Communist ideas of equality, democracy, and a better life resonated with many at a time when, in the shadow of fascism, human rights were oppressed.   For many, the Communist Party was the revolutionary hope for the future; however, for the majority, joining the Partisan Resistance Movement simply provided the means to fight Nazi fascism.

Italy surrenders.   Many former Italian soldiers join Partisan Resistance

Changes quickly occurred in July 1943 with the Allied landings on the island of Sicily, off mainland Italy, making the country's surrender imminent.   Benito Mussolini's regime was overthrown by the Fascist Grand Council and the monarchy. Italian King Vittorio Emmanuel III had Mussolini arrested.   An armistice was signed on September 8, officially declaring Italy's surrender.   Aware of the impending armistice, Nazi Germany immediately deployed troops into Italy, rendering the Italian military powerless.   The collapse of the Italian government brought chaos to the country.   The rank-and-file soldiers' situation changed before they understood what was happening. In an attempt to flee enemy fire, many Italian soldiers went into hiding. Thousands were captured and deported to Germany. Others across northern Italy, including many of the Slovenian minority who had been in the Italian military, now joined the Partisan Resistance Movement which, by this time had gained the Allies' support for its effectiveness in fighting Nazi fascism.

Arrival of occupying German forces

In his book *Valdirose*, Marcello Morpurgo vividly describes the rapidly changing scene as he witnessed it in Gorizia on the afternoon of September 10. German forces had already arrived in Salcano (Solkan in Slovene) on the outskirts of Gorizia. Tito's partisans, wearing red neckerchiefs, drove trucks with red flags through the streets of Gorizia, while Italian soldiers still guarded the bridge of the Isonzo River, waiting for orders which would never come. On September 12, the Partisan Resistance in Italy fought one of their first battles of the war at the train station of Gorizia when they collided with German forces.[19]

On that same day, Hitler had Mussolini released from prison and flown to Germany to consult on setting up the Italian Social Republic, a new Italian government with its seat at Salò on Lake Garda. A military corps was created to support the Republic and "to assist the occupying German forces in rounding up 'dissident Italian elements' behind the German lines and to render such other duties as might be required to throw back the invading Allies."[20]

Milena's region becomes territory of Nazi Germany

From September 1943 until the end of the war, the provinces of Gorizia, Trieste, Udine, Fiume (Rijeka), Ljubljana and Pola (Pula in Slovene and Croatian) on the Istrian Peninsula became the territory of Nazi Germany. The Adriatic Littoral area now became the new German province known as *Operationszone Adriatisches Küstenland*, (Operation Zone Adriatic Coastline, or OZAK), under the direct administration of Hitler's Third Reich. Following the Italian Armistice, Trieste native and notorious Nazi leader Odilo Globočnik was chosen to head both the SS and the police in OZAK. Under his command, and with the collaboration of those Italians who maintained loyalty to fascism, this period resulted in the highest number of arrests, executions, and deportations to Nazi concentration camps for the Slovenian minority in Italy.[21]

INTRODUCTION

The horrors of war do not end when the fighting stops. It was 1945. The Second World War was over. Bergen-Belsen concentration camp had been liberated by the British. Yet the death toll continued to rise. One young survivor named Milena, a Slovenian girl from Italy, lay in a hospital bed, delirious with typhus, fighting for her life. This survivor was my mother, and this is her story: the story of a young life filled with hardship as her family fought for freedom under fascism.

During my youth, I would sometimes open the top middle drawer of my mother's dresser and study the remains of a small, plaid diary. Its pages were ripped out, but handwritten on the inside was a French name—that of a former Bergen-Belsen prisoner. I would touch the faded burnt orange, yellow and tan cover, imagining the stories its contents could have told. My mother never really spoke to me in any depth of her experience at Bergen-Belsen, but occasionally she would mention this journal cover, the family members who never returned, and, of course, the vision. This, more than anything else, intrigued me: the vision my mother had experienced while suffering from typhus, in the throes of a high fever, the vision that had foretold her brother's fate. Throughout my life, I have often wondered whether this had been a prophecy or a hallucination.

Only after I began reading Holocaust survivor stories during my graduate work at the University of Rochester did I feel compelled to begin recording my mother's story. I was uneasy at first, apprehensive about hearing the tales that had remained locked away for so many years. As her story began to unfold little by little, I was amazed at the clarity of my mother's memories of her youth and war experience. Her narrative was far different from those I had read. It portrayed the life of a Slovenian family living on a border which had been long affected by political change. Although these experiences tell the story of one family, they represent the suffering of many Slovenes in Venezia Giulia.

The contrast between reality and my mother's altered state of consciousness is ever-present in the beginning chapters of this memoir. Although Milena does not remember, during the delirium of her illness, she had been seen running frantically through hospital corridors. On the other hand, she had had lucid moments which she recalls in vivid detail seventy years later. This confused state of mind defines the framework of Part I, with Milena narrating the events that shaped her eighteen years of life as they played out in her mind. These reflections convey the circumstances that led her family to adversity during the fearful era of Fascist Italy.

Part I

In Delirium

CHAPTER 1

The Vision

Early May 1945, sick with typhus in German military hospital near Bergen-Belsen

I awake with a start. The rolling sound of wheels along a hallway floor muffles a desperate cry, a faint moan from the other patients in my room. Stillness follows. I turn, feeling the scratchy sheets damp with sweat beneath me. As I glance down the long empty corridor of the hospital, my attention is drawn to a quiet stirring just outside my room. A group of people come into view, but they are not hospital personnel.

These figures move down the broad hallway in a solemn procession—a slow march of long black dresses, scarves and shawls hiding their identities; of black suits, hats politely in hand. They do not look my way. Those at the end of the procession are sobbing as they walk down the hall behind a wagon. On it sits a plain wooden coffin. I do not recognize any of the mourners, for their faces blur, as does the scene before me. Only the coffin remains in focus, and it strikes me with dread to imagine that within it lies my brother Pepe. They have killed him.

I am overcome with a deep sadness, believing in my heart that Pepe is dead. I close my eyes for a moment. When I open them the corridor lies vacant before me. My surroundings fade into blackness and I drift, remembering … remembering …

Milena's Childhood in Vrtojba, 1930s

"*Obrni ret*! Turn your bottom around," Zora squealed under the covers.

Bociada, we teasingly called her—always complaining about something, always ready to pick a fight.

"*Ti obrni ret*! No, you turn around," I shouted back, unable yet to roll my 'r'.

"Be quiet," Nino grumbled. Even half-asleep in the bed nearby, he resented sharing a bedroom with younger brother Milan and two younger sisters. Our childish mischief annoyed him to no end—after all, he, along with Pepe, his twin, were the firstborn, which Nino felt entitled him to a privacy we could not afford. While Pepe had moved to Ljubljana to work as a ceramic tile mason, Nino remained at home. Besides, it was Thursday, one of the few nights it was permissible to go courting. After spending the evening with his fiancée, Nino was especially irritated to have his sweet dreams disturbed by our rambunctious antics.

"Turn around!" Zora's squeal rang out in the darkness.

"No, you turn around!" I poked her sharply with my skinny knee under the covers. Although I was two years younger, I was determined to hold my claim to half of the little mattress we shared.

"I'll turn your bottoms around!" Nino shouted, picking up our mattress and flinging it into the air, throwing us beneath it onto the wooden bed frame. Zora and I lay there, giggling uncontrollably. Tomorrow Mama would freshen our mattress with the softest, most delicate inner leaves surrounding the cob, but tonight, because we had angered our brother, we had to sleep on lumps. I crawled from beneath our ransacked mattress and nestled next to Zora in our uneven bed.

Early May 1945, German military hospital

I am lifted out of a warm bed. Lying next to my sister was comforting, but a nurse carries me back to my own room. He speaks to me in German. I don't understand everything he says. "My sister—let me stay in bed with my sister," I cry.

"Das ist nicht deine Schwester. Sie ist eine andere Patientin." ("That is not your sister. She is another patient.") I understand only these words when he tries to explain. The room spins as he lays me in my own bed, alone.

"Where is my sister?" I think. The sheets are cool against my naked body. He puts the chair next to my bed and sits, my guard, preventing me from running free.

Milena's Childhood in Vrtojba, 1930s

I needed to run. Run and be free, as I had always been. As a child I felt akin to nature as I climbed the treetops, moving quickly from limb to limb, passing from tree to tree with squirrel-like agility. Our plots were fertile with vineyards and a rich assortment of fruits and vegetables. The town of Vrtojba, with its surrounding towns and countryside was our playground, and the excitement of Gorizia, the city, lay just beyond the fields that nurtured us. We dug tunnels through haystacks, played games around World War I ruins, and thrived on the unrestrained ingenuity of youth. Mama and Tata did their best to provide for us, but the growing number of children in our family made it difficult. I was the seventh child, and there were three more born after me. We were a *"famiglia numerosa,"* as Mussolini called us, one of the biggest families in Vrtojba, and it was impossible for my parents to fulfill all our needs.

Figure 2. The Gulin family in 1927: from left to right in first row, Vilma, Nona, Milan, Nono; second row, Pepe, Nino, Tata, Baby Milena, Mama and off to side, Zora and Stanko

CHAPTER 2

The End of an Empire

Gorizia (Görz in German) under the Austro-Hungarian Empire

Figure 3. The medieval castle stands high on a hill overlooking Görz, with today's Piazza Vittoria in the foreground, 1901. At that time the piazza was called Hauptplaz in German, Piazza Grande in Italian and Travnik in Slovene.
Courtesy of *Isonzo Soča, Giornale di Frontiera* (Postcard: Schloss, Stengel & Co.)

***

Gorizia and its surrounding towns,
including Vrtojba, were part
of the vast Austro-Hungarian Empire
under Emperor Franz Josef.
After WWI, this land was annexed to Italy.

***

Under the Habsburg Rule

Figure 4. A grand parade in Piazza Vittoria for Emperor Franz Josef's 1900 visit to
Gorizia to celebrate four centuries (since 1500) of Gorizia's rule under the Habsburg
Empire.
Courtesy of *Isonzo Soča, Giornale di Frontiera* (Foto: Musei Provinciali, Gorizia)

About my parents: 1914-1921, from Vrtojba to Mozirje and back to Vertoiba (Italian)

My parents, Jožef and Marija Gulin, lived under the rule of the former Austro-Hungarian Empire. Following tradition, Tata brought Mama into his parents' home in Vrtojba to live and raise their twins, Nino and Pepe. In that big house with its adjoining fields and vineyards, Mama settled in to create a home for her young family.

Figure 5. Tata and Mama as newlyweds

***

In 1914, the Austro-Hungarian Empire
declared war on Serbia. Germany and
the Ottoman Empire joined Austria-Hungary
against Serbia and the Allies.
Italy joined the Allies in May 1915.

***

Mama and Tata were newlyweds when the war broke out. As a citizen of the Empire, Tata was recruited into the military to fight for Austria-Hungary, leaving Mama at home, caring for the twins and helping out on the Gulin farm.

The Italian Allied force advanced on Gorizia and its suburbs to drive the Austrian army away from its position on the Isonzo-Soča River. When Mama described the event, her quivering voice exposed the terror she must have felt.

Told to me by my mama, Marija:
I was home alone with the twins on the day the soldiers arrived. Italian enemy troops were throwing grenades, reaching as far as Šempeter and Vrtojba, and our homes were directly on the front line. Austro-Hungarian soldiers passed from house to house, ordering everyone to leave immediately. The twins were sick that day. The farm animals needed tending, and just days ago the sow had given birth to a big litter of piglets. Unnerved, I threw what necessities I could

gather into a sack. We had no choice but to comply with the orders and leave everything else behind. Out on the street I found chaos, as ox-wagons and mules carried the townspeople out of Vrtojba, leaving terrified livestock and ancestral homes behind us in flames. In shock, with two crying babies in my arms, I joined the caravan of refugees being herded by the soldiers, and tried not to look back.

The journey was long and exhausting, but I experienced the good-heartedness of two Austro-Hungarian soldiers of Italian ethnicity, who helped me carry the twins by mule until we could be lifted onto a wagon. Nino and Pepe had diarrhea, and at night I slept on the ground beneath the wooden wagon, soothing my babies with breast milk. By morning, the yoked team of oxen resumed their slow but steady pace, pulling us along the winding dirt road through the countryside as we traveled two hundred kilometers through the Vipava Valley and northeast to the banks of the Savinja River. There we found refuge in the village of Mozirje-Šmartno ob Paki, where we remained within the Austro-Hungarian Empire until after the war, when it would be safe to return home to Vrtojba.

While in the military, Tata missed his family. His happiest times were visiting them in Mozirje. More than twenty-five years later, Mama revealed this secret about Tata to me. Speaking in hushed voice, Mama still expressed concern for Tata's wartime reputation.

> ***Told to me by my mama, Marija:***
> We were living in Mozirje when Tata shot himself in the finger in order to have a military reprieve. When days at home became weeks, his battalion noted his lengthy absence for what was considered an insignificant wound. Tata had never taken his responsibilities lightly, and did not then. Restless nights agonizing between spending one more day with us or fulfilling his military obligation wore him down. It was late on a wet spring night when we awoke to voices outside calling his name. Peeking through drawn shutters, we spotted several soldiers from his battalion. We knew our time together was over.
>
> Tata flew down the steps and jumped out a back window, finding shelter in a neighbor's stable. After searching the house in vain, the soldiers surrounded the structures in the vicinity. With pitchforks they poked the hay in the barns and nearby stables, stirring the farm animals from

their sleep, while Tata lay face down, holding his breath, praying he would not be discovered. Early the next morning he began the return journey to combat, and nine months later Stanko was born.

***

Austria-Hungary collapsed at the end
of the war in 1918, and the Peace Treaty
gave Italy territory that had belonged
to Austria-Hungary, including, Trieste,
Gorizia and its neighboring towns, such
as Šempeter, Bilje, and Vrtojba.
With the breakup of the Austro-
Hungarian Empire, Mozirje would
eventually become part of Yugoslavia.

***

The Gulin family wanted to return home to Vrtojba after the war, but the community in Mozirje encouraged them to remain longer. Tata had become comfortable there in his craft, making fine shoes, and the townsfolk did not want to lose their skillful cobbler. Mama soon gave birth to my sister Vilma, who, just as Stanko, was born a Yugoslav citizen.

When the family of six finally returned to *Vertoiba* (Italian), the Austro-Hungarian Empire was dissolved, and our homeland had been annexed to Italy. Although my family continued to use the Slovenian names for our town and those around us, under the Kingdom of Italy, all place names had been

Italianized. According to Mama, my parents discovered another change upon their homecoming. As the firstborn male child of his family, Tata was to inherit his parents' house and land, but because he had remained in Mozirje longer than expected, his brother Franz had taken up residence in the homestead. In amends, Tata's father gave him enough money to build a house, and Mama's father gave the money for the stable. Before long, our growing family took up residence a few streets away at 34 Čuklje Street.

Living under Fascist Italy, but longing for the old days under the Empire

Mama and Tata frequently told us of their contentment with many policies under Habsburg rule. The Slovenian people had the freedom to speak their language at home, in their towns and in the city of Gorizia. Under Franz Josef, German was the official language, but because the Empire included so many ethnic groups, families had the right to send their children to schools with classes in Slovene. Books and newspapers in their mother tongue were plentiful under Austria-Hungary, which explained how Mama and Tata could read and write so well in Slovene. By contrast, the Fascist State prohibited our Slovenian language to be spoken in public; and, under Italy, children were never allowed to receive an education in their home language. We all longed for the tolerance of the old Habsburg Empire.

CHAPTER 3

Milena's Childhood under Mussolini and Fascist Italy

***

In 1922 Benito Mussolini,
the Premier of Italy, transformed
the country into a totalitarian state.

***

Mama had already given birth to their fifth child, Marica, but due to growing Slavish discrimination under Italy, my parents were required to register her with an Italian name. Unfortunately, little *Maria* died before reaching the age of one. Milan was the next to be born in Vrtojba as an Italian citizen in 1922, then Zora in 1924, and I in 1927.

Mussolini hoped to transform us young Slovenes into loyal Fascist citizens. Since we were one of the largest families in town, we were eligible to receive certain privileges from the

State, such as an occasional welfare package, a gift from *La Befana* at Christmastime, and several months of summer camp for the neediest child in the family.

It was one such year that, compliments of the State, I attended summer camp. I was always the one chosen from our family because I was so little and skinny. Living so close to both the Adriatic Sea and the Julian Alps afforded us two possibilities. Sometimes we were sent to resorts to breathe the ocean breezes; other times it was an alpine environment for the crisp mountain air. This time we stayed at the seaside resort of Grado. Although I felt homesick, I soon adapted to the structured environment the Catholic Sisters had created for us. Each morning as the Italian flag was raised, we saluted in unison with the words, "*Viva il Re. Viva il Duce.*"

I did not understand every word they spoke in Italian, but I observed the others and quickly learned the daily regimen: the roll calls, the neatly formed lines, the meals at regular times, and the rows of beach towels where we children, at the nuns' command, flipped every fifteen minutes from our backs to our fronts and back again. They insisted we drench our skin in the sun in this manner twice a day, and by the time summer was over, our tanned little bodies appeared the picture of health.

The sisters marched us two by two into the center of Grado, to a store where we could purchase beach accessories or a toy to make our stay more enjoyable. Clutching the coins Mama and Tata had given me, I had time to consider my options while awaiting my turn. Upon noticing a basket of colorful balls, my decision became easy, and I anticipated buying my new *palla*.

But my hopes were dashed when the clerk didn't hand me the ball. Instead, he placed a *pala*, a small metal shovel in my hand. Clearly, I had not made myself understood in this new language.

One afternoon, a sister inspected our worn shoes and chose those children whose shoes were torn to form a line. What I lacked in the proficiency of Italian, I made up for by careful observation and strategy. I investigated and found the line led to a table piled high with numbered boxes. Although I was only five years old, I recognized opportunity. My shoes weren't torn, but hiding away from the line, I proceeded to rip them by the sole. Fearful they would run out of shoes, I quickly wedged myself between the second and third child in line. When my turn arrived, I was thrilled when the teachers reached for a new pair of white canvas shoes. As they pulled them on my feet, the teachers asked, "Do they fit?"

Although my lovely new shoes were so tight they pinched my toes, I knew if I complained, they would be taken away from me. "Oh, yes, Sister!" I answered enthusiastically. "They're perfect!"

At the end of the summer, the buses rolled into the city center of Gorizia, where parents awaited to reunite with their children. My father came to take me home on bicycle. He checked me out from head to toe, and when his eyes fell upon my feet, he exclaimed, "Those shoes are beautiful!" I felt so proud, but even more grateful as I rode high in the basket on Tata's handlebars, my feet too sore to walk any further.

Early May 1945, German military hospital

I try to raise myself from the mattress, but I am too weak. The nurse who has been guarding my bed hands me a cup of lukewarm tea. Suddenly I'm in the company of friends. It's so nice to see familiar faces. They've come to visit me. As they stand by my bed, I tell them, "This tea is bitter. Go downstairs to my mother and get some sugar. My mother is just downstairs. Go and ask her," I implore. But they just stand there, glaring at me. Why don't they help me? In vain, I try to drink, but it just drips down my chin. I feel myself fall back onto the bed.

Childhood in Vrtojba, 1930s

Drops, drops, drops of rain. As children, we were always happy to see the rain because, as it washed the ground, it exposed pieces of bombshells and shrapnel from WWI. After the rain, we went out on our foray with a big bucket and sometimes a long, thin metal stick which helped us to find the buried ammunition. We perused the fresh, clean soil for indentations which might reveal evidence a bomb had fallen at that location. We were elated whenever we found brass or copper, which was worth most of all. "Oh, look at this big piece!" we would exclaim as we crouched between the rows of grapevines. We would each go down separate rows in the vineyard, in order to cover as much territory as possible. We knew the neighboring farmers took a dislike to our trespassing because our footsteps would compress the wet soil.

One evening Milan and I had had a particularly successful forage. Our bucket was nearly full of shrapnel when we spied the owner. He followed as we ran downhill from the vineyard. By the time we entered the woods, he was just paces behind us. Milan was five years older than I, and in bare feet I struggled to keep up. He pulled me by the hand and then by my dress as I began to slip further behind. But the stretchy fabric of my wine colored frock caused me to lag more than a few steps behind, just enough for the owner to almost catch hold of my dress. With a quick jerk, Milan saved me from certain capture and, with the increased steepness of the hill, the man ceased his pursuit.

Catching our breath, we collapsed with relief at the top of the Šempeter (San Pietro in Italian) hills looking down on Vrtojba in the distance. When we recovered, we clambered downhill to the town shopkeeper, who bought shrapnel. After weighing each piece, we were delighted when he handed us five *lire*. We didn't tell Mama we had already stopped at the store to treat ourselves to some delicate slices of mortadella, studded with fat and slivers of pistachio, before strolling home to show her the remainder of what we had earned. She was so pleased to be able to refill the cupboard with a much needed liter of cooking oil that she sent us directly back to the store.

Both Mama and Tata were good cooks. I could almost taste the *minestra* and barley soup, the *polenta* with savory goulash, and rich risotto, which filled the kitchen with a sweet, steamy aroma. Only my oldest sister, Vilma, was allowed in the kitchen to help. Mama was so particular in her ways, she had never trusted the rest of us. I had always looked forward to Sunday dinner, which began with Mama's flavorful, beef *brodo* with tiny homemade pasta. The second course consisted of fried potatoes and seasonal vegetables. Mama would save the beef she had used to prepare the stock for the *brodo* and add it to a creamy risotto for our evening meal. We were thankful for the bacon, salami and ham from each of our pigs, but the meat usually did not last the whole year. We always had fresh eggs from the chickens, and on certain occasions we sacrificed a plump fowl for a special meal.

When we were young, there was seldom enough food. At the end of a meal Milan sometimes licked everybody's plate. Zora had to be watched too, since she was known to hide bread inside the trunk in the kitchen. Even so, mealtime was a happy time of day, and I often lingered in our warm, cozy kitchen until I fell asleep at the table and had to be carried to bed.

Because we were always hungry, food was the highlight of any experience. And so it was with *asilo*, or preschool, which I attended from the age of three to six. Each student was assigned a one-square meter plot and taught how to plant seeds and nurture a garden. I happily harvested my beans, garlic and onions. When we were lined up for our daily dose of cod liver oil, however, I was less enthusiastic.

At dinner, I always tried to sit next to children from small families. They usually ate more slowly, and some of their families even kept bees and brought sandwiches with honey. I ate with speed in order to be the first one finished. Then I would advise those seated around me, "Hurry, they're coming any minute to take our plates away. You'd better share your food with me because I can eat fast." They would usually comply, so I finished theirs too.

In first grade, on my way to school, Mama gave me permission to stop at the store to get a writing tablet, pencils and an eraser. My mouth watered as I stared at the big jars of marmalade that stood on the counter. For ten *centesimi*, the shopkeeper weighed an individual serving of marmalade and wrapped it into a piece of paper. "Put it on my parents' bill, please," I told the shopkeeper, unable to resist the sticky treat, even though I knew it was not the right thing to do. To avoid the possibility of someone telling my parents what I had done, I scurried to school without even attempting a taste on the way. The morning lessons seemed endless as I anticipated devouring my sweet gem. When it was finally time for recess, I hid in a corner of the schoolyard where, in constant fear of being discovered, I licked the marmalade from the paper to destroy the evidence.

As much as food was the high point of my early school days, the negative impact of first grade affected my whole academic future. Our community was an ethnic group that spoke Slovene, but because it had become part of Italy after World War I, we had to speak Italian in school. Within those walls, my Italianized name was *Emilia*. I couldn't comprehend everything the teacher said, and I had difficulty expressing all my ideas in this second language. When I was called up to the blackboard, I became nervous, knowing the teacher would strike my hand with her pointer if my answers were wrong. I dreaded the teacher's daily reminders that I was not wearing the required black apron with white collar, nor had I brought the five lire for school registration, plus one lira for the student report card which was due each year. I was afraid to go home and ask my parents for money I thought they might not have, but every day the teacher impatiently asked me the same question, *"Gulin, ha portato i soldi per la tessera?"* ("Gulin, did you bring the money for enrollment?") And each day my answer became harder to repeat.

As a result, I avoided school in any way I could. I created stories that I had to attend a funeral of an aunt or an uncle, and I spent as much time as possible hiding out in the countryside, where I practiced my writing with a stick in the dirt. My cousin Dora or my childhood friend Yelko often joined me in playing hooky. We were careful to duck into the gutter or lie flat in a field when we saw our teacher riding home on her bicycle after school.

When I was in third grade, I had to deliver dinner to my brothers, who were working in Gorizia. I watched the clock, so at precisely 10:30 each morning I could raise my hand to ask the teacher if I could run my errand. After a few weeks, my daily question must have worn on her nerves, for she finally pronounced, *"Va, va in nome di Dio!"* ("Go, go in the name of God!")

We children may have skipped school, but we were in attendance for every funeral in Vrtojba. Whenever Zora and I heard the church bells ring, we free-heartedly took off for the home of the deceased, gathering our friends as we raced through the streets, sometimes taking shortcuts through fields. Wide-eyed, with morbid curiosity, we watched the mourners as they sobbed in grief, and observed the procession passing by the coffin. Sometimes we got in line with the mourners to get a better look at the body. We indulged ourselves in anointing the body with Holy water, according to Catholic liturgy. In our enthusiasm, by the time we had each filed by, the body was dripping. Finally, after the casket was lowered, we all took part in the ritual of throwing a piece of earth onto the coffin. Being the smallest, I would climb atop the mound of soil next to the grave to throw the biggest clump I could find.

What I lacked in school, I made up for on the streets of Vrtojba. I was known as a tomboy and always tried to show my strength, for I never grew tall like my sisters and brothers. Only Stanko, who, just as I, had been born in the month of January, shared my small size. I was always trying to demonstrate my stature in other ways. I was proud of my reputation as the leader of our neighborhood gang and was determined to uphold it, so I acted tough. I could tell the others respected me, for when they saw me swaggering down the street, hands clasped behind my back, I could hear them whisper, "Here comes Milenka!"

My best friend, Yelko, and I had been like brother and sister since we were small. His family lived down the street near the well where Čuklje Street curves toward the main street of Vrtojba. They were well off, owning an *osteria* and lots of land. When we were little, he sometimes brought me a piece of bread, cheese or pork speck from home, or we would enter his family's barn and steal eggs from the hens. Then we broke them into the sand, pretending to make *polenta*. He would go into the *cantina*, where they stored beverages for the bar, and break bottles of soft drinks, just to remove the multicolored marble prize in the neck of each.

Yelko was always trying to please me. When we were about eight years old, he used to say, "I'm going to buy you a pair of boots and sunglasses." One day he proudly told me he was ready to purchase that pair of sunglasses. He must have stolen the money from home, because I had seen him earlier that day running from his house, throwing coins from his pockets into the hedge, with his mama chasing close behind.

Off we went to the city of Gorizia. Taking a shortcut through the farmers' fields, we walked hand-in-hand to the city center, passing by the stately villas of Via Vittorio Veneto on our way. "See that villa?" Yelko would ask. "One day we'll have a villa like that."

Near the *tribunale* building was the *tabacchino*, where cards, tobacco and sunglasses were sold. Together we looked through every pair of glasses until we found the most beautiful pair. Proudly wearing my first pair of sunglasses, we returned to Vrtojba through the winding cow paths of the countryside. Yelko's parents stopped their potato harvest to stare as we skipped across the fields, leaping over piles of hay.

Early May 1945, German military hospital

When the doctor makes his daily rounds, he stops to look at me. He walks to the foot of my bed, where he notes my condition. I feel as though the room is spinning.

Childhood in Vrtojba, 1930s

Spinning, spinning, spinning on a little red velvet stool with fringes that hung all around. I was only three or four years old when I accompanied Mama to deliver Tata's dinner to his shop on Corso Italia, the main street in one of the best sections of Gorizia. I remember the shop window, with its display of all the beautiful shoes. While I spun around on the stool, feeling the fringes tickle my legs, I could see the faces of customers looking through the window at the fine shoes. Tata had many good customers—Austrians, Slovenes and Italians, including members of the Jewish community. Mama often helped Tata by delivering the shoes to many of the beautiful villas in Gorizia.

Mama worked so hard. Always meticulous, she kept our home spotless, with no corner left untouched. Mama kept us children neat and clean too, insisting upon regular bathing, sending us to the barber well before our hair grew too long, and making sure we washed our feet before bed every night. While we played, Mama was often stooped over the washboard, scrubbing our clothes. She fussed over Tata too, always straightening his shirt collar before he left the house. Mama was a refined person, and she taught us to take pride in our appearance and to present ourselves in a respectable manner. As a dressmaker, she was often up late into the night with her own work, making sure her sewing always met her high standards. Her stitches were so fine that she had many customers in Vrtojba who placed more orders than she could handle for dresses, and even wedding gowns.

We children always had clothes handmade by Mama, and Tata used scraps of leather to make us new shoes and sandals. He even used discarded gentlemen's hats to make us the warmest and most beautiful slippers. Mama and Tata always worked hard to earn a living and take care of their big family.

My sister Silva was born in 1929. Now she was the baby and took my place sleeping between Mama and Tata, while I slept in the crib on Tata's side of the bed until I was almost six years old.

I felt close to my Tata and always wanted to be with him. After cutting the hay for the animals, I often rode in the wheelbarrow as Tata pushed it through the fields. He was tall and handsome as a prince, and I sat on top of the heap of hay feeling like his princess. Most of all, I wanted Tata to be proud of me. One time when I was about five years old, I went into the woods across from our vineyard to forage some much-needed firewood. Picking sticks from the locust trees to contribute to the family's firewood stock, I tied the fresh, thorny branches, which were not even suitable to burn, into a little bundle. I rushed to my father, who was working in the yard, proudly offering my gift. Appreciatively taking my bundle, without reproach, he stuck it high up on the fence.

Tata was known for his kind, gentle temperament. Despite Mama needing help with disciplining so many children, he could never bring himself to spank or scold. The best he could do was oblige Mama when she told him to catch us; even then, he didn't try very hard. Mama would say, "Go up and get her now. She's probably in bed." Hearing his footsteps on the stairs, I would hide down near the foot of the bed. In the dark, he would feel the covers in an attempt to locate me. I was so little, I often eluded capture. Tata, finding his search in vain, would begin laughing.

During the night, I always wanted to hold Tata's hand because I was afraid of the dark. He would put his hand between the railings of my crib, and I would grasp it tightly. We had overheard Tata talk to Mama about a mysterious force which occasionally haunted him during the night, oppressing him by holding down his body, not allowing him to move. Once I witnessed the phenomenon for myself. From my crib, I could tell Tata's sleep was disturbed that night. I heard him muttering, but his body appeared frozen in place. It sounded as though he was having a nightmare. "Now, she's gone!" he shouted, as he unexpectedly kicked his legs into the air.

I shuddered, remembering what some of our neighbors had said about the spirit: "*It* could even enter through a keyhole." A few townsfolk had made a connection between the spirit and the hunchbacked woman who owned the plot of land next to ours. For this reason, children occasionally followed the old lady, hexing her with their fingers and commenting about the black and blue marks on her body. "Looks like she was pestering people again last night and got beaten up," they would taunt.

I never understood what the mysterious force was, but it gave me reason to be afraid. Although I would wake up frightened during the night, knowing my tata was within arm's reach made me feel protected and allowed me to fall back to sleep.

Early May 1945, German military hospital

I awake in a sweat alone in the dark room. I reach out, but no one is there. The nurse is no longer sitting next to me. I've lost all sense of time. I close my eyes and remember Tata comforting me when I was scared. I wish he were here to comfort me now. I wonder if I'll ever see him again.

Childhood in Vrtojba, 1930s

My sister Olga was born in 1932. That made nine of us plus Mama and Tata. Since my older brothers, Nino, Pepe and Stanko, now had jobs in Gorizia, they were at home less often, but Mama still had her hands full with five of us, ranging in ages from baby Olga to Milan at ten years of age. At five years, I fell right in the middle. Luckily for Mama, my oldest sister, Vilma, was like a second mother to us. At thirteen years of age, Mama expected her to help take care of us; and she did, although we never really appreciated everything she did.

We all adored our youngest sister, little Olga or Olgica, with her big blue eyes and golden blonde hair. She was always with Mama as she went about her daily work. Mama loved to sing, and it was very cute to hear Olgica sing along as she helped Mama pick vegetables from the garden.

Early May 1945, German military hospital

I can see early morning light begin to pour through the window. Now I'm aware of the others sleeping soundly in their beds around me. But as fatigue overtakes me, I am enveloped in darkness.

Childhood in Vrtojba, 1930s

I lay in bed, remembering that tomorrow would be my turn to take the *tessera* to get our family's ration of bread. For as long as I could remember, there had been shortages, so we looked forward to using our *tessera*. My stomach rumbled with the thought of the delicate aroma of freshly baked bread.

I awoke before the rooster's crow, quickly dressed and scurried out of the house, the *tessera* carefully tucked into my pocket. The moon still shone dimly in the sky, giving way to daybreak. Mama said the *tessera* could not be used at the first bakery I passed, but only at Giordano's, the second store down the street. I licked my lips in anticipation, planning my next move. Early morning brought the town's women to the city, anxious to redeem their coupons. I lingered around the first bread shop, waiting for the baker to arrive on his three-wheeled bicycle to deliver his baskets of bread.

I saw him in the distance, walking toward the first bakery on his run. The aroma of the freshly baked bread was so enticing. While the baker was in the shop weighing his merchandise, I sneaked under the canvas covering the baskets on his vehicle and grabbed as many loaves as my hand could hold. Then I went on my way to Giordano's store, where our ration would be available.

The women had already gathered in the shop. "He must be here! I smell bread. The baker must have arrived," they muttered among themselves, not knowing the delicious aroma was coming from my bag. After getting my family's rightful share, I leisurely strolled home, enjoying my extra portion of bread.

What we lacked in consumer goods, we made up for in creativity. With the scraps of fabric I found from Mama's dressmaking and from the decorative turned-down tops of children's socks some relatives had sent us from Egypt, I sewed doll clothes for my homemade rag doll. Sometimes I even dressed frogs I caught in the creek behind the house. And yet, I longed for a real doll like some of my cousins and classmates had.

My opportunity arrived at the annual carnival held at the nearby town of Miren (Merna in Italian). I perused the merry-go-round and other amusement rides, but could not take my eyes off the toys for sale. At the end of one table, there stood a doll—a doll with blonde hair just like mine. She stared at me with her big, blue eyes as I passed by the display of toys again and again. Captivated by her beauty, I inched her closer to the edge of the table with each pass, until she simply fell into my half-opened umbrella. I ran down the hill to the *osteria*, where many of the town's children had gathered to try out their new toy cars and trucks on an empty table. When Zora saw me, few words were needed to express what had happened. She dashed off, and, not much later, emerged with a doll of her own, but one that was prettier and at least a head bigger.

I was so proud of my doll, and I took her everywhere with me. I named her Adriana and even baptized her. Now my rag doll remained abandoned in a corner, and the frogs in the creek, while I sewed dresses for my real doll. I understood my good fortune could not be repeated, so I never let her out of my sight—until the day I visited Cousin Dora. Dora wanted to go play in the garden. My doll sat next to me on the bench in the yard, and as I reached to take her along, Dora's older sister said, "Leave the doll here. She's fine sitting here. I'll watch her for you."

When I returned, my doll was gone. "I don't know where it is," she told me. "Maybe it fell into the toilet." But my doll was nowhere to be found. My initial shock led to sadness, and I walked home that day with a kind of emptiness never to be filled again.

Figure 6. Milena with younger sister Silva.

Figure 7. Milena in asilo sitting next to her teacher in the second row

Figure 8. Communion at church in Vrtojba. Twelve-year-old Milena stands alone in the second row. Yelko is the tallest boy standing in the back row.

CHAPTER 4

The Sting of Fascism

There was so much in our lives beyond our control, it made us feel powerless. Although we were only children, we felt the effects of the politics of Mussolini's Fascist State in our daily lives. Tata, like most Slovenes, was determined to fight for something better—freedom. But it did not come without a price. Because he refused to become a member of the Fascist Party, Tata was eventually forced to give up his business in Gorizia. By the early 1930s he closed his shop on Corso Italia, and from then on his shoes and cobbler's forms occupied a little room off our kitchen.

We lived in Italy and were Italian citizens, but our Slovenian ethnic group did not allow us the same opportunities as those whose primary language was Italian. In the city of Gorizia we were considered second-class citizens. When we walked down the sidewalks, we were reminded by the signs, *"Qui si parla soltanto italiano."* ("Here Italian only must be spoken.") It was forbidden to speak Slovene in shops and *osterias*. If we were heard speaking our native language, we were looked down upon and sometimes spat on.

Although my mother and father could speak some Italian, there were many old people, such as my nona and nono, who could not. My grandparents seldom went into Gorizia any longer, and when they did, they walked down the streets with their mouths shut. When they occasionally needed to tend to business at a municipal office, Vilma accompanied them. Once when Nona and Nono visited the post office, Nona did not understand the transaction. She looked toward her husband and Vilma for clarification. As Nono turned to her and spoke a few words in Slovene, the office clerk indignantly slapped him across the face.

My parents and grandparents never lost their fondness for the old Austrian Empire, nor their secret contempt for this new Fascist State. Within the city of Gorizia many of the people supported Mussolini and his policies, but we Slovenes in the suburban towns and countryside who faced discrimination were opposed to the Fascist regime. Yet expressing that opposition in public would have brought arrest.

Ethnic Slovenes longed for freedom and equality. Many in our area had experienced imprisonment and torture. If anyone was even suspected of working with the Partisan Resistance Movement, the fascists would often take their whole family away, leaving the house looted and sometimes burned to the ground. At home we heard our parents express their concerns about the fascists. We children lived in fear—some fears that had already been confirmed and others that filled our dreams with terror.

Some ethnic Slovenes escaped to South America, such as Tata's brother Venc, who, at the age of twenty, fled in the middle of the night to make his way to Brazil. Guštek, Tata's youngest brother, moved to Ljubljana, Yugoslavia. Mama and Tata, however, never spoke about leaving. With so many children, it would have been impossible. Instead, Tata thought and spoke about the revolutionary ideas of communism and a better future for us. It was important that such talk occurred only behind closed doors, because even civilians occasionally reported what they had seen and heard.

Many others were thinking and talking about communism also. On Sundays after dinner, the men in the neighboring towns gathered in the *osterias* to talk about politics. They played *bocce* and sometimes sang forbidden songs about freedom. After a few drinks and a heated political discussion, arguments often ensued. My father would sometimes lose his judgment and show loyalty to a friend by getting involved in fights that were not his own. He wasn't very strong, and he often ended up getting the worst of the beating.

Once he was arrested for his suspected opposition to fascism and spent several days in a basement at police headquarters in Šempeter, where the officers questioned him concerning his attitudes. Mama went to the jail and cried, "Please let my husband out. We have so many children at home!" This time Mama's plea was answered, but she lectured Tata sternly that from now on, he needed to be more careful in public.

Frequently by four o'clock on Sunday afternoons, my mother would tell us, "Go look for your father." Zora and I would take off on our brother's bicycle, with her pedaling as I sat on the front bar. We would start at the *osteria* down the street in Vrtojba. From there we went to the *osterias* in Šempeter and on to Bilje. Sometimes by nightfall, we had not yet found him. We would check the gutters by shining a flashlight on both sides of the street. We knew Tata did not drink much but got dizzy quickly, so if only a few friends offered him a glass of wine, that was enough to cause problems.

As we searched, we anticipated the difficulties we often had on Sundays. There was always arguing when he got home. Mama wouldn't sleep all night. Sometimes a friend brought him home and tried to get him up the steps to bed. I even helped push once, just wanting to get him to bed so we would have peace, but Tata was unaware and pushed me down.

One Sunday night, we came home without Tata. Mama paced worriedly all night. Fearing the worst, none of us slept. Soon after dawn, we heard the sound of Tata's bike on the gravel in the yard. Laughingly, he told Mama the story of how he had paid a visit to the tailor in Bilje to pick up some goods. They had stopped for a drink, and, instead of following the road leading home, he had turned the wrong way, in the direction toward the Vipava, a river with a current running fast and deep. By the time he had waded into the river up to his knees, the cold water had revived him, and he realized where his drunkenness had led him.

It was on one of those Sundays that our little sister, Olgica, had the accident. It was *Binkošti*, the holiday when many children are baptized in the Catholic Church. Although no one at our house had gone that day, it was a happy occasion for our neighbors who had already returned from church. We children were running in and out through the gates between the two houses. Mama was preparing the family dinner. Vilma usually watched us, but she had gone away with friends for the day. Olgica was crying at the gate, but she was barely two years old, and I, at the age of seven, as well as the others, did not want her with us.

Mama went to the garden to pick radicchio for dinner, and Olgica went with her as she usually did, singing her favorite song, "Ave Maria," with Mama. When Mama returned to the kitchen to clean the radicchio, she sat on Mama's lap. Milan was standing outside the door being a nuisance. He was blowing on the window and whining, "I'm hungry, I'm hungry! When will dinner be ready?"

Mama worked to prepare the meal as fast as she could. We children were still in the yard running around, causing a lot of commotion, while Olgica quietly slipped off Mama's lap. "Go see where Olgica is," Mama told Milan. But Milan was still carrying on at the door with his antics and did not obey. When Mama insisted, he finally went.

All of a sudden, we heard Milan's piercing cry. We ran through the yard just as he was pulling Olgica's body over the wall from the cesspool below. It had just been cleaned and was mostly liquid, but some excrement had remained. Olgica must have seen us stand on the wall to urinate, as we did occasionally instead of using the outhouse, but she would have been unable to hold on to the iron peg we older ones had used to keep our balance. She must have lain in that liquid waste for at least several minutes. During the time we had been running around the yard from the house to the garden and creek, past the wall and back into the yard and through the gate again, none of us had noticed Olgica's little blue dress floating in the murky pool.

Mama grabbed her baby and shook her as she cried and screamed. Olgica began to vomit, and we all watched in horror as excrement, even from our goat, fell from her choking body. Mama continued shaking, crying, screaming. Within a few minutes, it seemed that half the town had gathered in our yard to witness this scene and offer support. Immediately, someone rode on bicycle to Gorizia to summon an ambulance. The *Croce Verde* arrived soon after, and as it sped away down the Čuklje, Milan clutched the wrought iron fence supporting his trembling body, sobbing uncontrollably.

Mama stayed at the hospital with Olgica day and night. We could see the relief on Mama's face as the baby gradually began to get better. We were all delighted to hear Olgica was so well, she could now jump up and down on her hospital bed. Mama doted over her and made sure the nuns did not keep the windows open to cause a draft. Nino went to visit her in the hospital, and even took her a little doll.

Unfortunately, Olgica's recovery was only temporary. By the following week, her condition had worsened. The doctors said she had an infection and there was nothing more they could do. Mama did not want Olgica to remain in the hospital. Taking the shortcut through the fields from Gorizia, she carried her dying baby home.

I looked at Olgica as she lay peacefully in her crib next to Mama and Tata's bed, her pretty blonde curls cascading around her shoulders. Those big, blue eyes stared at me, even though she could no longer really see.

They laid Olgica, or *Elvira*, her registered name according to Italian law, out in a little white casket on the table in Mama and Tata's bedroom. I still remember where I sat at the dinner table after the funeral, and how good Mama's *brodo* tasted.

That wasn't the end of the story. After the accident, the authorities were going to arrest my mama for negligence, because the law required that a cesspool be closed if there were children around. The cesspool had been emptied just a few days earlier. The goat manure, and the excrement from the chickens, along with the human waste from the outhouse, had been pulled out and taken to the fields for fertilizer. Usually after being emptied, tree limbs were placed across the hole, but this had not yet been done. Because Olgica had been considered recovered from the accident, the police did not press charges; but if the baby had died sooner, under Italian law, Mama might have gone to jail.

With Olgica's death, sadness came over the whole family. Although they went through the motions of living, Mama and Tata were not the same. Their torturous grief began to affect our family. Milan blamed himself for Olgica's death, but Mama seemed to blame Vilma most of all. If she had not gone out with her friends that day, she would have been there to watch the children. Just as many young girls often went away to work for the wealthy, Vilma, soon after Olgica's death, left home for Milano, Italy to babysit for a doctor's family. She probably would have gone eventually, but being only fifteen, the guilt over Olgica's death caused her to leave a few years sooner than expected. She didn't return home for two years.

We all missed Vilma, as she had helped raise us. I regretted more than ever the time when, at the age of four or five, I had pushed her down the stairs. I remember her long, brown pigtails as I came up behind her and, for no reason, gave her a shove. Losing my balance, we tumbled down the stairs together. I was bleeding, but luckily Vilma was not injured. Because Mama had always taken for granted that whoever got hurt was never guilty, she presumed Vilma was to blame. Mama grabbed her by the pigtails and hit her in the corner of the kitchen. Instead of telling our mama what had really happened, Vilma accepted the consequences of my action.

We had never taken a picture of Olgica. After her death, whenever Mama saw pictures of angels on postcards, she saved them because she said they looked just like Olgica. And all the songs Mama and Olgica sang together, we never heard Mama sing again.

CHAPTER 5

Happy Events and Prosperity

After Olgica died, I happily reclaimed the crib she had occupied in order to be next to Tata's side of the bed. One night I awoke feeling paralyzed, as though a force was lying on top of me preventing me from moving my legs. I remembered Tata had experienced this force. I tried to call out for him, but found I could not speak. Before panic overtook me, I kicked my legs with all my strength and *It* went away. I was free.

Olgica had been gone for four years by the time Mama gave birth to our youngest brother in the summer of 1938. Being eleven years of age, I was old enough to understand what was happening as I listened from my bed that night, hearing Tata's quick footsteps up and down the stairs as he accommodated the midwife's requests, and finally the cries of a baby shortly before midnight.

It was a special gift to have a baby in the house again. We argued over what we would name him. We finally decided to call him by the Slovenian name, Darko, but as the rest of us, he needed an Italian name to fulfill the requirement under State law. For that purpose, Mama chose the name *Luciano*, but in the end, she liked the name so much that we all called him Lučano at home too, and Darko became his middle name.

Nino was almost twenty-five when Mama gave birth to Lučano, and he and his fiancée, Lucija, were soon ready to marry and begin a family of their own, so he was embarrassed that Mama had a newborn. A few weeks had passed, and Nino, who had managed to ignore the birth, had not yet met his new baby brother. After sewing a beautiful sky-blue dress matched with its finely-worked cap to present as a gift for the baby's Baptism, Lucija finally convinced Nino to see Mama and the baby.

Lučano was a healthy baby, but not too long after birth, Mama noticed there was a milky secretion coming from his breasts. A bit alarmed, she talked to friends and neighbors around Vrtojba about the problem. Some blamed it on the mysterious force. Was it the same force that had occasionally disrupted Tata's sleep? Did *It*, too, find its way through the keyhole at night? My questions were never answered, but the townsfolk advised Tata to stick a knife through the bedroom door in order to make *It* go away. And it worked—as mysteriously as it had appeared, our baby brother was now free of the problem.

On Nino and Lucija's wedding day, I was in bed with bronchitis and a high fever. In the evening, as customary, the whole family was having dinner at the home of Lucija's parents, but I was home alone. As the groom, Nino should have stayed with his bride on their wedding day, but he came home to see how I was doing. Even though we occasionally annoyed him, Nino really cared about us children.

The newlyweds slept at the home of Lucija's parents, but spent their days with us. Although we already had a full house, Tata welcomed Lucija into our home and insisted we treat her with the utmost respect. She was also a dressmaker, and she set up her sewing machine by the front window of the parlor. Tata had taught Nino his trade of shoemaking, and he claimed a corner of the kitchen near the stove for his equipment. They were much in love, and we often caught Nino gazing out the kitchen window as he watched his bride carry water home from the town well down on Čuklje Street.

As we got older, the household was easier for Mama and Tata to manage. Pepe was serving in the Italian infantry, and Stanko was usually working away from home. Vilma had returned from Milano, but she too was always working—first as the chef at an orphanage and later at the marmalade factory. Milan and Zora had jobs now too. Silva and I were the only children still in school, and Baby Lučano got attention from all of us. The Gulin family was complete with nine children, and we were growing up and beginning to form our own lives.

Mama seemed more content as she busied herself with the household chores. Sometimes there was even a smile on her face as she walked down to the creek to wash the clothes. Tata spent long days harvesting the crops, and we all took pride helping around the house and in the fields and vineyards.

One day during the harvest, Tata cut himself on a piece of wire fencing while spreading the hay to dry in the warm September sun. He had injured himself many times before, so he paid no attention to this mishap, but continued to complete the day's work. It was not until a week later that Tata showed Mama his sore ring finger. Topical medicine had little effect, and day by day we watched Tata become more uncomfortable. Soon his finger had swollen to double its size.

Mama hired a woman in Vrtojba who cured patients with all sorts of maladies. Over the next week, she made daily visits to shave the skin around Tata's finger in hopes of reducing the infection. But the pain had grown so unbearable, Tata was no longer able to sleep. Although my brothers set up a bed for him in the downstairs parlor, during the night his cries of pain still rang through the house. After the swollen finger had turned a grotesque purplish-brown, Mama realized the town woman's "remedy" had not worked. By the time Tata had finally gone to the hospital in Gorizia, gangrene had set in, and the only solution was amputation. Tata's wound eventually healed. From then on during planting season, we smiled whenever Tata seeded our plot of land. Without that finger, near the middle of each freshly seeded row, an empty line stretched across the field.

I was home the day Tata walked in and laid the bag of money on the kitchen table. I had never seen that much money at one time. Because Tata made a living partly from agriculture, the government had reimbursed him for his disability. With that windfall, Mama and Tata paid off all the bills, purchased land,

and even had money remaining to buy our first cow. Now we no longer drank goat's milk, and for the first time in our lives our family felt financially comfortable.

CHAPTER 6

World War II

***

Italy entered the Second World War
on June 10, 1940 with the Axis Powers,
alongside Nazi Germany.

***

Although life had improved for the Gulin family, our country was soon to be thrust into war once again. Bands of soldiers marched into the mountains with equipment and mules to practice military maneuvers. Even before the war had broken out, Yelko and I used to get caught up in the excitement by following soldiers partway up the winding paths through the hills as they sang their routing Italian Alpine song, "La Penna Sul Cappello." We sang along ...

Sul cappello, sul cappello che noi portiamo,
(On the hat, on the hat that we wear,)

c'è una lunga, c'è una lunga penna nera,
(There's a long, there's a long black feather,)

che a noi serve, che a noi serve da bandiera,
(That we use, that we use as a flag,)

su pei monti, su pei monti a guerreggiar. Oilalà!
(Up in the mountains, up in the mountains when we fight. Oilalà!)

Su pei monti, su pei monti che noi saremo,
(Up in the mountains, up in the mountains we will be,)

coglieremo, coglieremo le stelle alpine,
(We will pick, we will pick edelweiss,)

per portarle per portarle alle bambine,
(To take, to take to the young girls,)

farle pianger, farle pianger e sospirar. Oilalà!
(To make them cry, to make them cry and pine. Oilalà!)

Su pei monti, su pei monti che noi saremo,
(Up in the mountains, up in the mountains we will be,)

pianteremo, pianteremo l'accampamento,
(We will pitch, we will pitch camp,)

brinderemo, brinderemo al Reggimento,
(We'll drink, we'll drink a toast to the Regiment,)

Viva il Corpo, viva il Corpo degli Alpin! Oilalà!
(Hurrah for the Troop, hurrah for the Alpine Troop! Oilalà!)

Evviva, evviva il Reggimento!
(Hurrah, long live the Regiment!)

Evviva, evviva il Corpo degli Alpin!
(Hurrah, long live the Alpine troop!)

Evviva evviva il Reggimento!
(Hurrah, long live the Regiment!)

Evviva, evviva il Corpo degli Alpin!
(Hurrah, long live the Alpine troop!)

Figure 9. Photo taken by Yelko of fourteen-year-old Milena on Cuklje

Even as we got older, my friends and I still loved walking up into the hills to look down upon the countryside. Yelko or one of the other boys would carry the bricks and skillet, while Dora, Olga and I carried the flour, milk, eggs and marmalade— all the ingredients to make *omelettes*. We gathered sticks and started the fire. We laughed, talked and sang songs, reveling in the fun and carefree life of youth. We joked about the priest at our local church and the way he would interrupt his sermon to yell at Dora, Olga and me as we sat in the last pew, whispering about what we would do after Mass.

Although I did not take the Church seriously, I followed its teachings by attending Catechism and Communion. As long as Yelko went through the motions of ceremony along with me, it was tolerable. The culmination was *Cresima*. On that occasion, Yelko's family hitched the horse to their carriage to pick up my godmother, Lidia, and me at home. Dressed in white with Bible in hand, I stood by the gate in joyful anticipation, watching the approaching mare make her way down Čuklje Street. Yelko and I sat high in the carriage together as the horse clopped its way to the baroque church in Piazza Vittoria in Gorizia.

Figure 10. 18th century baroque church Sant' Ignazio in Piazza Vittoria, where Milena was confirmed. Built by the Jesuits, construction began in the late 1600s and was completed in the early 1700s.

We joined the Catholic Church together that day, dressed up in our formalwear with our families looking on proudly. After the formalities, we celebrated at a nearby restaurant owned by my father's uncle. Then we continued our trip in the carriage all the way to Šempas, where Yelko's relatives lived, to further celebrate the happy day. By nightfall, as we rode back to Vrtojba, the horse was so weary Yelko's uncle had to walk alongside her, pulling and coaxing her step by step.

Figure 11. Fifteen-year-old Milena dressed for Cresima with godmother, Lidia

Although I had always lived in the fear of fascism, the reality of war and its brutalities had not yet penetrated my mind. While the horrors of war inched closer into our world, we still experienced happiness in our daily lives. Nino and Lucija gave birth to a baby girl named Jolanda. Mama and Tata were delighted to become grandparents, and we had our first niece. It was also fun for our brother, Lučano, to play and grow up with a little niece who was of similar age.

I felt a void in our home after all my brothers had been drafted into the Italian military. Nino served in the army, which took him to Russia. The infantry sent Pepe south around Arezzo, and Milan, also in the infantry, was sent down to Sardinia. Stanko, who was an aviation mechanic in the Air Force, did his military training in Northern Italy before being sent to Sicily and further south to the island of Malta. My sisters were busy working also. In addition to her job at the marmalade factory, Vilma worked as a housemaid. Zora found a job at the cotton factory.

I, too, had begun to consider finding work, when Olga told me about an available job as a nanny for a rich fascist family in Gorizia. Unsure, yet wanting to contribute money to our household, I decided to give it a try. With Olga by my side, we walked down Corso Verdi to the cross-street where the palatial building stood. The fine architectural details and the intricately carved doors belonged to an era when a wealthy family lived in this house as a private residence, but it had since been divided into several luxurious apartments.

We walked up to the entrance and knocked on the massive, wooden door. The woman of the house greeted us, and together, we explained the purpose of our visit. She led us through the cobblestone-paved entrance to the beautiful garden behind. Encouraged, we listened as she proceeded to describe the duties of caring for her infant son, and, to our amazement, she ended her list of responsibilities with a job offer. Looking to Olga, who appeared stronger and more mature, the woman waited for a response, but Olga pointed my way and replied, "Oh, I'm not looking for a job; she is."

The woman looked me over with apprehension. "Do you think you can handle the work?"

"Oh, yes. I have a little brother at home, so I know what to do."

She offered me the job on a trial basis. I was to live with the family in their fancy apartment. She was an Italian from the South, and her husband, a smartly-uniformed high officer of the Italian Air Force. Although they lived in the heart of the city, the yard behind the house, with its fragrant flower gardens and towering trees, was home to a variety of birds and butterflies. It was late summer, so during the day I put the baby in his carriage and sat outside to enjoy nature. Unfortunately, the job did not go according to plan. He was a fussy baby, and my patience soon wore thin. When he cried, I pushed the carriage around the yard and shook it back and forth, but nothing I tried made that baby stop crying.

To make matters worse, my bedroom faced the street, and I wasn't accustomed to the noise of the city. "By day the baby does nothing but cry. At night, the city traffic keeps me awake. What am I doing here away from home?" I asked myself as I lay in bed that first night, unable to sleep. I longed to be home in my peaceful town, surrounded by the green countryside.

In the morning, I told the woman that my mother had contacted me and wanted me to return home. "You've only made the sheets dirty," she indignantly replied.

As I walked out the door and stepped onto the sidewalk, I felt free again. Relieved, I scurried through city streets toward Vrtojba, taking a shortcut through the fields and vineyards, stopping to sample some plump, juicy grapes, ripe for the September harvest.

It was still morning when Mama saw me walk through the gate empty-handed. She was in the yard with Pepe, who had come home on leave for a few days. "You're home already?" she calmly asked. I felt as though I had failed her.

Pepe was busy chopping wood, but when he saw me, he put down his ax and proclaimed, "Good that you quit. You should never work for fascists." His solidarity warmed my heart and reminded me that, for a day, I had compromised my dignity for the sake of money.

* * * *

That winter, Lucija contracted pneumonia and spent time in the hospital, leaving Mama to care for both Lučano and Jolanda, our niece. Poor Mama was always running up and down the stairs, catering to everyone else's needs. After taking some *camomilla* tea to Jolanda one night, she slipped and fell down the flight of stairs. By the time she tumbled to the bottom, she could hardly breathe. The strain of life had taken a toll on Mama.

Because Mama and Tata had so many sons serving in the Italian military, Vilma's employer, a high-ranking *carabiniere*, eventually made it possible for us to submit a request for Nino's discharge. While in Russia, Nino's troop had marched hundreds of kilometers through bitter cold and snow. Several comrades had died along the way from the brutal conditions. Nino walked many kilometers across the frozen terrain to return to his new family. We were all relieved to have him home again.

* * * *

The townspeople in the suburbs of Gorizia were always under suspicion by the Fascist regime. On more than one occasion, police came to question town residents about the whereabouts of their male family members who had failed to register in the Italian military. Their suspicions were warranted. Throughout the area, many young men were beginning to join groups of partisans in opposition to the Fascist regime and its alignment with Nazi Germany. Although ill-equipped to fight, their numbers grew steadily. Eventually they were to become a formidable force in the Resistance Movement.

My friend Olga's brother, Slauko, who camped in the nearby mountains, was suspected of being a partisan. The fascists gave his family twenty-four hours to get him home or all face arrest. Near midnight of the following day, my father heard the sound of an army truck roaring through town. He raced for the attic and crouched at the small window to peek onto the street below. Seeing the truck pass by, heading in the direction of Olga's house, confirmed that Slauko had not returned. We were not surprised when we learned the whole family had been taken from their home. They were being held in a room at the Seminary of Kostanjevica.

I remember it well because my brother Stanko was to be married the following day. It was a small, discreet wedding since his bride, Ana, was expecting, so only Vilma and Milan

74

witnessed the vows along with Mama and Tata. Fourteen, foolhardy and left to my own devices, I hiked up the hill to the seminary where Olga's family was imprisoned to see whether I could at least catch a glimpse of her. I spied her face peering out of a second-story window, but a wall surrounding the seminary prevented us from doing any more than wave to each other. I wanted to shout out to her, but at that moment I heard footsteps marching up the gravel path. Afraid of being arrested for suspicious behavior, I slid down the sloped bank by the church and hid in the bushes until I saw them pass—fascist soldiers, guarding the prisoners. I never told my family where I had been that day. My thoughts were focused solely on what would become of my friend.

We later learned that Olga and her family had been sent to a camp down south near Naples. They returned a year later to their empty home to rebuild their lives. The fascists had looted everything: furniture, personal belongings and even the farm animals had been stolen. Although Olga had been away for a whole year, it took little time for us to renew our friendship.

* * * *

By the time I reached the age of fifteen, I was beginning to appreciate clothes and fashion. I had always admired Mama and Lucija for their craft, and had wanted to be a dressmaker like them since I was a young girl. Mama tried to discourage my interest. Hoping I would learn from her experience, she would say, "Don't become a dressmaker like me. You'll have to work so hard, even on Sundays. Think about your life. You'll never have any freedom."

However, my determination eventually wore her down, and she gave me permission to begin sewing lessons. I persuaded Olga and Cousin Dora to join me, so together the three of us became apprentices under Lucija's competent supervision. Our families called us "the three soldiers" because we often wore dresses Lucija had made for us from the same fabric.

***

Benito Mussolini visited Gorizia
on July 31, 1942.

***

We Slovenes who lived in the countryside around Gorizia knew ourselves to be considered second-class citizens. However, for those of us who had grown up under the Fascist regime, there was no other reality. Therefore, when Mussolini came to Gorizia on an official visit, we joined in the excitement. I met my sister Zora on Corso Verdi, where people had gathered in anticipation of Mussolini's procession through the city. She, along with the other workers, had been given time off for the momentous occasion. Pushing our way through the crowds to get a better look, we saw Mussolini. He was standing proudly in the open vehicle. His stern demeanor accentuated his hard features. He looked my way and, with raised, outstretched arm, saluted as he rode by. I saluted back.

CHAPTER 7

Under Hitler's Third Reich

***
In July 1943, the Allies land in Sicily.
The Armistice is signed on
September 8, officially declaring
Italy's surrender. On September 10,
German forces arrive in Gorizia.
They occupy northern and central
Italy, including Venezia Giulia,
which becomes part of the
OZAK German territory.
***

I'll never forget the date, September 8, 1943, when Italy surrendered to the Allies. The radio in the nearby osteria was our main source of news, so when the announcement rang across the airwaves, word spread quickly through town. A feeling of euphoria filled our hearts. We were free.

The Italian military collapsed. The soldiers who had been in the army went wherever they could to escape the Germans. They gathered in the streets of town, not knowing where to hide. Their abandoned mules roamed through our fields hungry, searching for food. Soldiers asked townspeople for clothes before attempting their journeys homeward, hoping to look like civilians and thus avoid capture. Others assembled at my school in Vrtojba to meet with a group who recruited them into the Partisan Resistance, and they fled into the mountains. Along the streets could be found discarded ammunition, and Tata and his friends gathered whatever they found near home to give to the partisans. Everyone was simply trying to survive in the midst of confusion.

Many soldiers, including my brothers Stanko and Milan, wanted to return to their homes in the North to join the Resistance fighters, the partisans, who used guerilla warfare to fight the Germans. Milan encountered a difficult journey from Sardinia to make his way north to escape and join the partisans. Stanko, however, was not so lucky. Along with many other Italian soldiers, he was captured and sent to a POW camp in Germany. We had not yet received any news about our brother Pepe.

The Italian military personnel had abandoned their stations, and the soldiers their barracks. This vacuum turned to chaos as military sites were plundered. When Zora and I learned about the looting in Šempeter, we hurried to forage whatever our family could use; however, we were among the last to arrive. Other families had already carted away enough supplies to remodel their homes. Having no wheelbarrow or wagon to transport whatever loot remained, we were limited to what we could carry. Shots from the hillside above let us know we needed to make haste. Running past airplanes still in their hangars, we entered a large storeroom and found a small bookcase, a wooden table large enough for our family, and several cans of airplane paint. Balancing the cans and the bookcase on top of the table, Zora and I positioned ourselves at each end and headed for home. As bullets flew past us, we shouldered our heavy load through the fields to Vrtojba.

No sooner had we returned home than we learned the partisans had taken control of the base. We wasted no time in arranging our newly acquired possessions. The table and bookcase fit perfectly in our parlor. We buried the cans of paint in the garden to hide the evidence. Sometime later, when we retrieved our paint, we discovered most of it had spilled, but just enough remained to paint the shutters of our home a very dark, very military green.

* * * *

After several months, we learned that a family in Arezzo had allowed Pepe to hide in their *cantina* in exchange for working in their gristmill. Longing to return home, he stole a ride by rail, face-down on top of the cars. He arrived in Šempeter with cuts, scrapes and tattered clothes from the wires that had snagged his body as the train sped along. Before he reached home, townspeople had already spread the word through Vrtojba that Pepe was on his way.

Pepe had been home only a short time, with no intention of joining the partisans, but an unexpected visitor changed all that. I was outside in the yard when I noticed a tall, well-built man walk through our gate toward the front door. Uninvited, he entered. Curious to learn more about the intruder, I followed into the kitchen. The man, pistol in hand, was holding Pepe at gunpoint. While I could not take my eyes off the weapon, Pepe sat in a chair near the cupboards, head down. Their voices were hushed, but I heard the person say, "You're coming with me." I could tell by Pepe's posture he did not want to go, but with the pistol still pointed at him, he had no choice. The stranger led him out the door, and all I could do was watch, not knowing when—or if—I would see my brother again.

* * * *

I had grown up fearful of the fascists, and now, with the Germans advancing toward our region, my fear was even greater. Rumors of the terror and killing by the Germans had spread from town to town. We had heard that if they suspected someone of being affiliated with the partisans, they would kill their whole family. Rumor had also spread they had killed all baby boys in the towns through which they passed. Mama was terrified for five-year-old Lučano when she heard this. The mere thought of losing another child was more than she could bear.

In the fall of that year, the reality of war entered our lives. I was out in the yard eating grapes from our fall harvest when I saw Vilma returning from her new job at the foundry, earlier than usual. Racing on her bicycle toward home, she cried out, "The Germans are coming!"

Townswomen emerged from their homes with looks of disbelief on their faces. "How do you know?" they muttered.

"I saw them in Gorizia!" Vilma replied, out of breath, as she turned into our opened gate.

Several hours later, as we hid in our home with shutters drawn, we heard the tramping of soldiers marching down our street. With no warning, Mama sprang from her chair and ran into the street, falling to her knees in front of our gate. Peering out the window, we watched with horror as the German troops came to an abrupt halt. Mama began to beg and plead, "Don't harm my baby … please don't harm my child."

Without speaking, a soldier shoved her aside with the stock of his rifle. My strong Mama had never appeared so frail as when she toppled over onto the ground, as the soldiers marched on by.

Soon after that day, the Germans began setting up camp in the hills across town. As more German troops infiltrated the area, the familiar sound of the comings and goings of townsfolk throughout the countryside was frequently interrupted by the roar of planes overhead. The partisans were located in the hills surrounding the towns, and the house where their meals were prepared sat above, in clear view of the enemy. The Germans' shots from an adjacent hill sailed across the towns and fields toward the partisan structure, piercing the peace of daily life.

The German presence in our lives caused us constant distress. Their stray bullets occasionally killed or wounded unsuspecting farmers as they went about their work. Sometimes a civilian, upon seeing a group of German soldiers approaching, would be shot when running for no reason other than fear. We quickly learned to restrain our actions, innocent as they might be, lest they be interpreted as suspicious.

As fighting intensified, bombs fell over the towns in our valley very close to our home in Vrtojba. We worried for ourselves, for our home; even that Roša, our poor frightened cow, might be trapped inside a burning barn. As bombs flew overhead, we led the restless animal from the stable across the creek behind our house. Tying her to a fence where she could reach the water, we left her between Čuklje Street and the main street of town that ran parallel. Lucija had some relatives who lived on that same street. That location appeared safer since the bombs were overshooting it, landing nearer Čuklje Street. Several other families had found refuge there from the danger overhead, and together in that house, we hid away for two days. Throughout Vrtojba, others did the same. No one left their safe quarters because they were afraid the Germans would kill anyone in sight.

We were especially distraught when we learned Zora was at the partisan house, where she volunteered for kitchen duty, as this was right where the bombs were falling. Tata wanted to go up and bring her to safety, but Mama refused to let him leave.

It was the middle of the day when we heard soldiers in the streets calling out, *"Wo sind die Leute hier? Hier ist keiner? Kommt alle raus, Leute, kommt raus! Wir tun euch nichts."* ("Where are these people? Nobody's home? Come out, people, come out! We won't harm you.") Having lived under the rule of Austria, our parents understood their shouts. Peeping through louvered shutters, I saw the soldiers in their helmets carrying rifles. In the distance, a tank slowly moved forward down the deserted main street. Not trusting their intentions, no one stirred further. We listened to the echoes of their laughter as they marched on through Vrtojba, which for those two days of intense bombing resembled a ghost town. The partisans dispersed from their hillside site, fleeing throughout the mountains to find shelter in caves. On the hills between there and Vrtojba, only splintered remnants of trees remained.

CHAPTER 8

Partisan Resistance

We were relieved to learn Pepe was alive and well. His visitor that day had been a partisan squad commander, who accompanied Pepe home on several subsequent occasions. Sometimes only the two of them came, other times the whole partisan patrol of five, including his friend, Vilko. We believed Pepe must have been brainwashed, since, despite his initial reluctance, he became so good at patrolling the area and spying on the Germans.

Pepe returned home often with his patrol. They would arrive around midnight or one o'clock in the morning. The Germans would patrol up and down the streets of town. It was dangerous for all of us when Pepe arrived with these four men on his squad, armed with machine guns and hand grenades. Tata was frightened when, after leaving their ammunition in our house, they used to walk around Vrtojba to the private homes where the Germans were having parties. While Germans danced inside, the patrol wrote political graffiti on the outside walls of the houses to demonstrate their ubiquitous presence. We stood at the windows, listening for signs of trouble. Whenever Mama heard a shot, she would shudder and cry out, *"Oh, Marija Devica!"* ("Oh, Virgin Mary!")

Straining to hear every sound, we would wait in the darkness, fearing they would not return. Afraid the Germans were coming down our street, Tata would grab the ammunition and run down to the creek behind the house to hide it in the bushes. I thought it daring the way Pepe and his patrol would sometimes hide from the Germans by jumping over fences from one neighbor's yard to the next, entering our house just minutes after the German guards had searched our street for them. We lived in fear, for we knew if the Germans had found them, they would have killed us all.

Even though we were fearful, we supported the Partisan Resistance fight for freedom from Nazi fascism. The ideals of equality and social justice invigorated our spirits. There were partisan meetings every week, during which decisions were made as to how each of us could contribute to the cause. Vilma cooked for them in the nearby town of Renče. In addition to cooking, Zora worked as courier, delivering messages to the partisans. Not knowing how to knit, I assisted by carding and spinning sheep's wool. From the spun yarn, those who could knit made socks and other garments to keep the soldiers warm. Farmers in the area supplied them with meat. Everyone in town seemed eager to do his part to help the Resistance.

One morning, my friend Olga needed to deliver a message to her brother Slauko, so she suggested we go up into the hills where the partisans camped. Since the walk was long and the summer day hot, our first stop was in Šempas at a house that stood high on a knoll, where Pepe's patrol sometimes met. There we refreshed ourselves with water. Before we could resume our trek, however, we heard a commotion from the road below and ran back inside. Peeking through closed shutters, we were astonished to see a German battalion, complete with trucks and cannons, passing across the valley road.

With a renewed sense of danger but an even greater thirst for adventure, we continued our march, far up into the mountains of Lokve. Olga guided the way, since this was not the first time she had taken this route to where Slauko and the partisans camped. We trudged over rocky terrain and brush on cornhusk sandals we had made ourselves, a true test for the durability of our handiwork.

Up in the beautiful forested area, we were surprised to see an Englishman in uniform riding past us on horseback. He was so out of place. We thought perhaps he had parachuted from a plane.

It was almost dark by the time we reached the partisan camp, where at least a hundred tents stood in a clearing. Olga and I stayed the night in one of the tents, eating beef *brodo* and potatoes that tasted uncommonly good after our long hike. Despite the signs of war all around us, the partisans found time for diversion that night. A room of an abandoned schoolhouse nearby was transformed into a dance hall, where a few partisans played their accordions while others waltzed and tangoed with female soldiers to the music. Olga and I couldn't help but be excited at this opportunity to meet boys. Olga danced much of the night, but no one asked me.

As we left the next morning, we proceeded with extreme caution, as Olga's brother had warned us there were many fascists hiding in the nearby hills. Although we arrived safely, our sandals did not survive, leaving our feet scraped and sore. I knew Mama and Tata would not be happy I had gone, but the pleasure of the company and the thrill of adventure had made it all worthwhile.

* * * *

When my enthusiasm for dressmaking proved to be short-lived, Vilma persuaded me to take a job where she worked, at the foundry in Gorizia. The Germans had control of all industry. Being at war, the foundry was of great importance to cast molds for airplane parts. My job was to straighten the nails that went into the molds. I didn't have a bike, and after six weeks I grew tired of the long commute, so I quit. Since our land was now under the direct administration of the Third Reich and everyone from the age of fourteen was required to work, the Germans assigned me the job of digging bunkers. At the end of each day, we were given tickets indicating the number of hours we had worked, and every two weeks we received our pay. Now I could work closer to home and would no longer have that daily walk from Vrtojba to the city. Olga also liked the idea, and, although we complained about the manual labor, in some ways I preferred working outside in the fresh air to that boring foundry job.

Zora was still working in the cotton factory in Gorizia. She had saved enough money to buy a bicycle, which made her commute easier, but her real passion was her job as courier for the partisans, delivering messages to Pepe and his patrol. While I admired her dedication to the political cause, it was obvious her interest included seeing Pepe's friend Vilko. When she spoke of him, her green eyes widened and sparkled in a way that told me she was falling in love.

The survival of the Partisan Resistance Movement was dependent upon secretly recruiting support from industry. Although companies were under the control of Nazi Germany, the partisans were sometimes able to coerce an administrator to yield to their expectations. Vilko persuaded Zora to arrange a clandestine meeting between her director in the cotton factory and the patrol. It was held at the director's private residence in Gorizia, where the partisans convinced him to supply their troops with materials to aid the cause.

The partisans also kept an eye on suspicious activities of ordinary citizens. When people in Vrtojba or the surrounding towns associated with right-wing Italians or Germans, it was brought to the attention of the patrol. In one case, a Slovenian girl was going around with an Italian Boy. Although Pepe had limited control over his commander's decisions, he was able to dissuade the patrol from harming the girl. However, in the case of a distant relative, Pepe had little influence.

Twenty-year-old Katarina had worked for the Resistance for some months, but later accepted a job as a typist in German headquarters. Townspeople reported she spent so much time with the Germans, she often returned home well after midnight. Her behavior made the partisans fear she might reveal information regarding their activities or meeting sites. Katarina represented a serious threat to the Resistance Movement.

I had heard about her disappearance, but knew nothing more until my friend Nevenka shared the rumors of Katarina's death. I did not want to believe it, but Nevenka not only insisted it was true, but was willing to offer me proof. She led me up the hillside into a wooded area. Nearing the spot, she pointed and whispered, "It's here."

With the head of the axe I had carried to cut firewood, I began to gently pull the earth toward me to prove her wrong. I expected to find nothing. Faster and faster I dug through the loose soil, until the hole I had made was about a third of a meter deep. Nevenka helped, and before long the moist earth beneath the locust trees lay in a mound between us.

"If they had buried her here," I thought, "her body would lie at least a meter under the ground." Concentrating on a smaller area, I dug still deeper. A few more scoops of the axe revealed a form. Gently pulling back the remaining soil exposed a bare breast, still plump from the moist earth. My shock and disgust were replaced by panic as we heard the voices of Katarina's mother and younger sister climbing up the woodland path. "A mother's instinct bringing her to this very site," I thought.

In a flurry of terror, we pushed the soil back over the grave. We dove into a hollow of brush, where we lay still until they passed. We didn't emerge until our bodies had stopped trembling.

As we made our way down the path toward home, we were aware of the possible consequence of our curiosity. If we had been seen, the desperate mother would surely inform the Germans, who would kill my whole family. When I walked into my house, the sweet aroma of Mama's *pasta e fagioli* filled the kitchen. Normally my mouth would have been watering, but our discovery had ruined my appetite for even this, my favorite meal.

CHAPTER 9

Captured

Pepe and his four partisan comrades always arrived without warning to elude the Germans whose patrol had become a frequent presence in Vrtojba. One day, however, Pepe showed up alone, pacing with restlessness because he knew the Germans were only minutes away. "Go and get me some matches!" he shouted.

"No," I replied, angry at the way Pepe tried to order me around. In an act of what could only have been madness, he fired a shot directly over my head, piercing the kitchen wall behind me. This jolted me into submission as nothing else could have.

Hearing the shot, Lučano raced down the stairs into the kitchen. Pepe, visibly shaken, dropped his pistol and rushed to embrace him. With eyes darting around the room, he whispered to our littlest brother, "I'm fighting for you, not for myself. For me it's too late."

Without a further look at either of us, Pepe picked up his pistol and dashed out the door. In an instant, I heard him jump over the fence. That was the last time we saw our brother free.

* * * *

Zora was the first to learn about Pepe's capture. Vilko was supposed to have been guarding the bridge that night, so she was puzzled when she learned Pepe had been captured there. The *Decima Mas*, an independent fascist military corps, found Pepe guarding that post, fully armed, and he was imprisoned in Gorizia. Working with the Germans against the Allies and the Partisan Resistance, the *Decima Mas* was known for its criminal violence and torture.

Mama sent me to the jail to pick up Pepe's clothes and bring them home for her to wash. Later I found her down at the creek, scrubbing encrusted blood from his clothes with tears streaming down her face.

Pepe had a nice-sized wardrobe, as he had spent several years working in Ljubljana before the war, but Mama found a note in his shirt pocket telling her he wouldn't need them anymore, and to pass them on to Milan. I wondered what Pepe knew of his fate that he had not revealed.

Since the German occupation, people sometimes traveled furtively to towns outside our area. Travel without a pass was risky, as it appeared suspicious, but the Germans did not give permission passes without what they considered good reason. So one day in May of 1944, it was with hesitation that Tata promised to accompany a friend, Jožef Gorkič, to Dornberk, a town about ten kilometers away. Jožef had promised Tata that if he came along, he would plow our field in return. We didn't own any equipment or even bulls, so we had to plow by hand. Jožef's equipment would make the job much easier, so Tata, even knowing the great risk he was taking, agreed.

I was there when Tata arrived home to tell Mama he and Jožef were taking the wagon to get some barrels of wine. Mama immediately scolded him for even thinking about accompanying his friend so far.

"Don't worry," Tata responded, "We won't be caught." Showing his burlap bag with an empty two liter bottle inside he added, "I'll bring some wine home, too. In this bag, it won't break."

Crying, Mama begged Tata not to go, "You won't come back! We'll never see you again!"

But our father was stubborn. Even though he knew Mama might be right, nothing could dissuade him. He had given his word to Gorkič and refused to take it back. So in spite of Mama's insistence, Tata left that day.

By evening, he had not returned. Mama paced the kitchen as she waited, fearing the worst. We heard voices on the Čuklje—disturbing voices, bringing news we did not want to hear. The Germans had a truckload of captured prisoners in Šempeter. They had come from those towns back in the hills— the area to which Tata and Gorkič had traveled that day.

Coincidentally, that same day, Zora had been near Dornberk delivering messages to the partisans. She had learned of the commotion in town, and, disregarding the potential danger, flew on her bicycle to see. As she approached the scene, she was distraught to discover Tata was among the men who had been caught. In an attempt to exonerate him, Zora shouted, "That's my father! He's innocent." The Germans simply pushed her aside, threatening to arrest her too if she continued to protest. Falling down beside the road, Zora watched in horror as they herded the men into the truck and drove away.

The German truck had been en route to Gorizia with its captives when two men escaped by jumping from the truck and hiding in the bushes around Šempeter. We heard from residents of Šempeter who had witnessed the incident that Tata was not one of them. In retribution, Tata and the remaining men were first lined up against a wall to be executed by shooting. Instead, they were beaten. These witnesses told us Tata had received much of his beating with the stock of a rifle to the head. He was thrown into the truck, conscious but suffering greatly from the trauma. It was soon confirmed that Tata, just as Pepe, had been imprisoned in Gorizia. Jožef Gorkič, who had been one of the escapees, was still free, but not for long. After discovering he was not Gulin, but Gorkič, the Germans had visited his family, threatening to kill his baby boy if he did not return home. So in that way, Jožef Gorkič was made to come out of hiding and was imprisoned along with our father.

We later learned the story of how Tata and Jožef Gorkič had been captured. A German patrol had stopped them in Dornberk. When asked what they had been doing in that town, Tata had honestly replied, "We are just getting wine for the *osteria*."

Tata had felt nervous as they began to search them. Earlier that day, Gorkič had shrewdly told Tata, "Hide my partisan pass in a safe place." Tata had obliged, folding it into a strip he had hidden under the band around his hat. He knew that if the partisans had stopped them, the pass would have been an asset. However, under the scrutiny of the enemy, a partisan pass would only label them as partisan sympathizers or even spies. To make matters worse, Tata's first name was also Jožef, so when they searched him and discovered the pass, they assumed Tata was Jožef Gorkič. We wondered why Tata had agreed to hide the pass on his person, allowing himself to be framed in the worst possible way.

Tata was in jail for just over a week when we learned he was being sent to a camp in Germany. We townspeople knew nothing about the camps in Germany. Just as Olga's family had been encamped near Naples for a year, we assumed Tata would serve his time in a similar type of camp.

The prisoners departed from the railroad station in Gorizia. We gathered all Tata's belongings, including his umbrella. Vilma, being the oldest and the one most trusted, was sent to communicate loving words from Mama and the rest of us.

The tearful cries of families calling their good-byes, the pungent smell of coal exhaust mixing with an atmosphere of desperation, created confusion on that unsettling late spring day. Vilma found Tata weak and distressed, yet, as the guards herded the prisoners toward the loading dock, she and Tata were somehow able to exchange important words of farewell.

Tata told her, "See that you all take care of everything at home. Now it's time to cut the wheat, and the alfalfa is almost ready to cut, too. Feed the cow and make sure the alfalfa is stored so she has food for the whole year. Try to keep up with it until I return." Tata turned his head toward the train that awaited him. Tearfully looking back, he repeated, "Try to keep things up at home so you can survive until I come back . . . because I'll be back. I have to come back."

Sobbing, Vilma now stood alone, watching Tata, bruised and disheveled, being pushed toward the cattle car. In one hand, he carried the bag we had so carefully packed; in the other, his umbrella.

Figure 12. Milena at seventeen years of age

CHAPTER 10

Arrest

Our lives had changed so quickly. Tata was gone. Pepe was in jail. Stanko had been captured and encamped. Nino and Milan were fighting with the partisans. Mama had always had so many mouths to feed, but now our *"famiglia numerosa"* had dwindled to Vilma, Zora, Silva, Lučano and me. We girls struggled to keep up the farm according to Tata's instructions. We cut the wheat and the alfalfa, and because it was still spring, there were more vegetables to plant. Plowing the fields was a challenge, as we had never done so before. Still, determined to survive, we did what we had to do. It was a busy summer for us all, going to work as well as tending the farm. By September, our hard work in the fields and vineyards had produced a successful harvest. We were proud of ourselves, and knew Tata would be pleased too.

Over the summer, Zora had become increasingly infatuated with Vilko. Even though her job as courier placed her in risky situations, she began visiting the partisans more frequently. On a September day, she rode up to Šempas on a borrowed bike to spend some time with Vilko, but the two lovers had an argument, and Zora was too proud to remain. Angrily, she hopped on the bike to head home.

Determined to make her stay, Vilko chased after her. Over and over he implored, "Don't go home. Stay here. It might be dangerous." But Zora was never the type of person who gave in during an argument. Headstrong, she rode toward Bilje, the town just before Vrtojba through which she needed to pass.

Zora never arrived home that night. Bad news always spread quickly through the towns, so we soon learned about the *rastrellamento* that had occurred in Bilje. The Germans had come to town to search the houses. During these raids, anyone caught on the street from another town without a pass was immediately arrested. Zora was thrown into a truck, along with that borrowed bicycle its owner never saw again. In this way, yet another member of the Gulin family was sent to jail in Gorizia. By the time the weather turned cooler and fall was in the air, Zora, too, had been transported to Germany. I wondered whether she would be living in the same camp as Tata.

Mama's sorrow grew as our family, one by one, was being taken away from us. By now, most families in Vrtojba had experienced similar loss. We all waited with hope for the American ground troops to advance beyond Bologna into our region. In the meantime, British and American planes bombed railroads and important buildings around Gorizia and Solkan. There was no escape from the sounds of war. Each plane overhead, the sounds of shots and bombs, and the alarms that startled us out of a deep sleep allowed us no respite.

Olga and I grew weary working for the Germans. With shovels and picks, we dug away the ground in the hills around Vrtojba to build German bunkers. Although we were used to hard work, by the end of December, colder temperatures made the job unbearable. Each day we reported to our assignment of digging through the vineyards of a house on the hillside. Throughout the day, Germans and others climbed that hill to seek refuge inside from the winter chill. The mother and two daughters who occupied the home grew used to the constant invasion of privacy. Several times each day, we too, walked the short distance to stand before the flames of their kitchen stove. This not only warmed our bodies, but raised our spirits as well. With fingers no longer stinging from the cold, we resumed our digging.

Once a young German soldier offered us a cigarette in the comfort of that kitchen, and for a few minutes we forgot he was the enemy. Yet, in the presence of the German colonel who traveled about the zone on his black horse inspecting our work, this soldier's demeanor quickly became less congenial. From then on, we were careful to be on our best behavior whenever we spotted that officer nearby.

Unfortunately, it became apparent that the residents of the home had already reported our frequent hand-warming. The Germans immediately assumed we were uncooperative laborers and began calling us "*Banditen*," as they referred to anyone they thought might be affiliated with the partisans. We were ordered to report immediately to the administration building at the airport complex in Gorizia.

We entered the palatial structure built under the Fascist regime, but now occupied by the German forces. Olga and I were led into an opulent office with marble wainscoted walls, where we found ourselves eye to eye with the colonel in charge of the zone—the one who rode the black horse. We stared across the wide mahogany desk, trying to anticipate the questions he might ask. For a German, he spoke Italian quite well. We were relieved that, after some routine questions about our activity on the job, he excused us. We returned to work the next day, determined to be more cautious.

January brought frigid days and even some snow. With no gloves to protect us, our cold-numbed hands lured us back to the comfort of that stove. Our activity did not go unnoticed. Minutes later, a German soldier shouted at us. I saw Olga respond to his words by raising her forearm and inserting her opposite hand into the crux of her elbow, meaning, "Go to hell."

Dumbfounded, I recognized the risk she had just taken with both our lives. Eyes downward, I shoveled away at the soil, hoping he had not noticed, but minutes later he came to inform us that we were required to report to the airport the following day. "And beware for your families if you do not," he added.

It was my eighteenth birthday. I feared it might also be my last day of freedom. Although we longed to avoid whatever dire fate awaited us, Olga and I knew that failing to report was not an option. The Germans knew who we were and where we lived, and they would not hesitate to come to our homes and shoot everyone. We had no choice but to report as ordered.

Despite our fear, on that ninth of January, we decided to celebrate. Yelko, Olga and I spent the evening at her aunt's house playing *Briscola* until midnight. Although I was scared, I didn't blame Olga for her moment of rebellion. Perhaps the officer would have had us report to the airport anyway, for the Germans collected information on anyone involved in the Resistance Movement. Because our brothers were partisans, we knew we might also be suspected of working against the Germans.

Morning came too quickly. As Olga and I walked together through the fields to the airport, deep in my heart, somehow I knew this time we would not go free. Upon reporting, we were disheartened when we were escorted to the same colonel we had seen ten days earlier. He was certain to recognize us. He made no mention of Olga's rude gesture, but instead began by asking us about our job duties and why we had performed them inadequately. I was not surprised when the interrogation soon shifted to politics, and he accused us of not working because we were partisans. "*Banditen, Banditen!*" he repeated. That word resonated in my ears. That hateful word, stripping us of any dignity. Reminding me of my place in this world, first under the fascists and now the Germans.

In an attempt to interject reason, I added, "But we only went to warm our hands in order to continue working. Our hands were so cold."

"There is no excuse," he replied sharply.

Two soldiers then escorted us to a building near the back of the airport complex. Formerly a horse stable, the long building was now being used as a warehouse. We were locked in an empty room filled with the smell of fresh hay that covered the floor. There was a tiny window high above near the roofline, through which we could occasionally hear the voices of German officers going about their business. But later that day a different sound broke the silence—the voices of our mothers, crying out just outside the door in the hope of seeing us.

How I longed to see Mama, to tell her how sorry I was for the pain I was causing. She did not deserve to suffer the loss of yet one more child. But all Olga and I could do was listen to our mothers' mournful cries.

Time passed slowly in that dimly lit room. Although we slept on the hay-covered floor, the winter dampness penetrated our bodies. We received no food or water, but the soldiers let us out twice to relieve ourselves behind some bushes. Thoughts of my family raced through my mind. Now only Vilma, Silva and Lučano still remained with Mama. I felt scared, and wished only to be home.

Late morning on the second day, we heard the sound of approaching footsteps. Soldiers harshly pulled us out and led us to a truck parked near the gate of the complex. The kitchen, where they cooked for the officers, was located nearby. A tantalizing aroma emanated from the partially opened window, where I spied the cooks staring out at us. While we were pushed into the back of the truck, a friend of ours, who had been assigned kitchen duty under the German occupation, stood at the doorway watching. As the truck drove off toward the jail, we were glad someone could tell our families where we had been taken.

CHAPTER 11

The Jail on Via Barzellini

I spent the next forty days in jail, sharing a cell on the top floor with about ten other female Slovenes, who had also been arrested for what the fascists called "political reasons." Metal cots with straw-filled mattresses lined the crowded cell, and in one corner hidden by a curtain sat a bucket, which we all used to relieve ourselves. The nuns brought us bread and water, a cooked meal daily for dinner, and also provided limited medical care as necessary. Two barred windows in our cell supplied a source of fresh air to alleviate the stench of too many bodies in a tight space. One window overlooked the street. Directly across the street, I could see the carriage shop that supplied and prepared transportation for funerals. I watched the carriages leave to transport coffins of the deceased to the cemetery.

Olga and I found the other window more interesting, for below we could view the prison courtyard. From our cell, we searched for the British actress who, inadvertently caught in a raid in a nearby town, now also found herself imprisoned on Via Barzellini. Although we had never spotted her in the yard, we passed our time peering out the window with that purpose. Standing on the windowsill, hanging from a bar that ran horizontally across the top, gave us the best view. However, each time a nun passed our cell, she yelled for us to get down.

I knew my brother Pepe was in solitary confinement, located in the basement. I needed to communicate to him, not only that I was there, but also news about our family. Although I was still hungry, I used my bread to send a message. Cutting a hole in the piece of bread, I carefully pulled out the middle. On a tiny scrap of newspaper, I then wrote my message, telling him of Tata's and Zora's capture and that they had been sent to Germany. My message contained no political content because, unlike my older siblings, I really didn't understand much about it. Neatly folding the piece of paper, I stuck it into the hole and carefully replaced the inside of the bread. To further conceal my message, I spread some marmalade on top. Then, with trepidation, I asked the nun if she would kindly give the bread to my brother in solitary confinement, since he needed more nourishment than I. And in that way Pepe not only learned I was in jail, but he received news about the family.

A few weeks after Olga and I arrived in jail, we were taken to SS headquarters to be interrogated. From the jail on Via Barzellini, we were led through the city, past the *municipio* and down Via Mazzini. We walked side by side, directly in front of a German soldier with his rifle over his shoulder. I felt ashamed walking down the streets of Gorizia with the soldier behind us, embarrassed I might be seen by someone I knew. Wishing to be invisible, I avoided the gaze of others who were going about their daily routines of work and shopping. As we walked down the sidewalk, I thought of running into a store to get away, but I knew we could not escape. That choice would have brought death to our families. I needed to endure the shame rather than put my family at risk. These were the streets I knew so well, yet accompanied by that soldier, I may as well have walked the streets of a foreign land.

Turning left onto Via Crispi, we soon arrived at German SS headquarters. The beautiful building with its well-appointed offices was in harsh contrast to my jail cell. Individually we were led into a room, where several officers sat around a huge, finely polished wooden conference table. I felt small and intimidated in the presence of these well-groomed men in their rich surroundings as they began to ask me why I had been imprisoned.

"I don't know why I'm in jail," I responded.

"You didn't perform your duties on the job! And tell me, where is your father?" one of them questioned.

"My father went to work in Germany, like some people do."

"No lies," they replied. "We know all about you. And what about your brother? Where is he?"

"I don't know where my brother is," I lied, knowing he was in the basement of the same jail as I, being beaten every day.

"Aha! No more lies, or we'll hang you up on that chandelier," another shouted, motioning toward the ceiling. "Look up there! If you lie, we will hang you up there!"

111

They said nothing about my other brothers. Apparently they had no information on them yet. I was thankful for that. We were led back to the jail on Via Barzellini in the same manner, and for the first time I felt relief in being hidden within that cell, away from public glances. If they had understood how little I knew, they would have known questioning me had been a waste of their time.

Our remaining weeks in jail became monotonous. We kept track of each day. A newspaper delivered to our cell painfully reminded us there was life outside those walls. Except for a petite teenage girl named Vilmica, who the nuns allowed to deliver the papers, no one left their cells. Time seemed endless. Our cellmates and we, all of us Slovene, quietly shared the stories of human misery under the fascists and Nazis, who had collaborated to create an atmosphere of terror for anyone suspected of opposing them.

Meanwhile, my body had also taken a toll from the filthy conditions of the jail cell. From my hands and between my fingers to my feet, I was covered with *scabbia*. The boils had formed yellow pus, and when I removed my bracelets, the scratching irritated my forearm. The nuns took me to the infirmary, where they scraped my whole body with a flat wooden instrument to open the boils and remove the pus. Tears rolled down my cheeks as I cringed in pain. My body burned as they applied a dark-colored ointment to my raw and swollen skin.

On one of my last days in jail, the nuns brought me a package from my mother. Although the guards would not permit family visits, they occasionally accepted deliveries of clothing and personal belongings for prisoners. Inside, carefully wrapped, were some sanitary napkins Mama had made for me. Embarrassed and angry, I put them aside, not wanting anyone in my cell to notice. Knowing full well I had not yet begun menstruating, I felt Mama was humiliating me. Was she reminding me that I, unlike my friends, had not yet become a woman?

The day arrived that we were released from our cell. Downstairs and into the courtyard of the jail we were herded. For weeks I had had the perspective of staring down onto the yard, but now that I stood on its soil, I felt uneasy. When the Germans lined us up to be counted, I knew we, too, would be going to Germany, although I naively hoped that, with arms and legs still unhealed, I might not be sent.

I was aware that I stood very near to the area of solitary confinement where Pepe must be. Although we had to stand at attention, I glanced back and spotted him peeping at me from the small basement window of his cell. Pitifully, he whispered in my direction, "Oh, poor child . . . now you. Two are already in Germany . . . Tata, Zora, and now you."

Careful the guards would not notice, I quietly responded, "You'll be going to Germany too."

But Pepe gave me a tearful look and replied, "Oh, no, I'm not going."

Through an acquaintance who worked at the jail, Olga's family had learned about the date of our departure, and having spent almost a year as prisoners near Naples, her family was knowledgeable about preparedness for camp life. Thanks to the recent slaughter of their pig, a relative delivered a pan of pork lard to the jail so Olga would be able to fry food at the camp in Germany.

On the other hand, my family remained unaware of our departure until the last moment. When they finally heard about more prisoners being taken to Germany, they didn't know whether it was Pepe or I who was leaving. It was my sister Silva who first arrived at the jail on bicycle, asking which one of us was being sent. After answering her, the guards wouldn't allow her to approach to give me the suitcase my family had packed. *Carabinieri* pushed her away and took her bicycle. As families cried their final good-byes, giving suitcases to their departing loved ones, Silva frantically stood by, unable to accomplish her mission.

Amidst all the commotion, I felt confused and frightened. The bus pulled up directly to the front door of the jail and the guards began to push us on. Just as I had entered the bus, Vilma seemed to appear from nowhere with my suitcase. With her tall stature, she was able to toss it through the bus window just behind me. Chaos ensued as family members tried to shout last words to us.

From the window, I noticed Silva had crowded with the others, trying to get near. I quickly scrambled closer. The engine had started, and with my arms extended, she was almost within reach. Then I saw that in her hands she carried food to sustain me for my transport. Crying, she ran with all the speed her body could exert, trying to keep pace with the roaring bus.

Following down Via Barzellini she chased the bus, trying to hand me the food. My arms strained, attempting to grab it from her outstretched hands. The bus turned right and drove about fifty meters. We were in front of the *tribunale* by the time our fingers met, and she breathlessly thrust the *omelettes* into my waiting hands. With marmalade oozing from them, only a few pieces of dough remained. The rest had spilled onto the street and floor of the bus. I watched my sister fall to the curb, sobbing uncontrollably. Apricot marmalade dripped down my arm. Our bus rumbled forward through the city streets, and although I could no longer see Silva, her pitiful image remained etched in my mind.

CHAPTER 12

Transport to Germany

Unlike Tata, we did not board the train in Gorizia. Because the American and British planes had done substantial damage to the rail system between Gorizia and the border of Austria, the bus took us over mountain passes all the way to Villach, just across the Austrian border. It was from there we began our transport by rail. Another bus had brought prisoners from the jail in Trieste to unload at the same station. Staying together, Olga and I recognized familiar faces amidst the confusion. We spotted Vilmica, who had delivered newspapers to our jail cell. Just as we, she had been arrested for political reasons. We also saw Jožica, from Bilje, who had been in the same jail. She and Pepe had been partisans together, and from our conversations, I thought perhaps they had been more than just friends.

Armed with rifles, the German soldiers herded us like animals, shoving us off the buses toward the waiting train. I was terrified. Flat cars loaded with army trucks, tanks and munitions were being hitched to the line of cars. Although the Allies' bombing had destroyed most of the rail network to Austria, it was apparent the Germans thought this train loaded with enemy equipment would not be bombed if we civilians were aboard. We were squeezed into a foul-smelling cattle car with straw-covered floor. A small, high window let in limited air and light. In this cramped space, about sixty of us would struggle to survive.

The train made its first stop in Austria that night. After a short time, they allowed us out of the car to relieve ourselves. The fascists took orders from a German commander who told them to guard us. Jožica, Olga and I, who had been put into the same car, stood in the dark of the starlit night, glancing at one another. Still in a state of shock and terror, none of us even mentioned escape.

On the second night, the train stopped and, after a lineup and count, the fascist guard complied with our request to relieve ourselves. This time Jožica, Olga and I gradually moved away from the rest. Our quiet whispers to one another revealed that each of us had considered escape. "What should we do? Should we try?" we asked one another in hushed tones, discovering our disorganized thoughts lacked any plan other than, "Now it's night. Why don't we run?"

With the guards watching us from afar, we had little time to strategize. Surely, if we had been aware of our destination, many of us would have attempted escape. Under the circumstances, we quickly evaluated the risks based upon the facts we knew at the time. If we did not make it and we were found by the fascists, we would be shot. How far could we have gotten? There were Germans and fascists everywhere. My thoughts went quickly from risk of escape to abandoning my belongings. Everything I owned was in that suitcase: my clothes, the beautiful plaid jacket Lucija had made for me. It was my first fine-wool jacket. We had gone to choose the fabric together—shades of red, gold and other beautiful colors. Cut on the bias, it fell so cute at the hemline. Losing that jacket would have been almost like losing my life. We agreed that leaving our belongings behind was too much of a sacrifice. Under the watchful eye of a guard, we made our way back to the line.

We were still in Austria when the train stopped again. We were at the camp of Mauthausen. A few cars carrying male prisoners had been unhooked from the train. Under the commander's supervision, the *Kapos* unloaded the men from our transport. We recognized some of them as fathers of boys we knew from Sant'Andrea, on the outskirts of Gorizia. Some of their wives, who were in my car, cried when they realized their husbands were to be separated from them. One of these elderly women died as our transport continued on its way.

It should have taken only several days to get to our destination, but it turned out to be more than a week. Inside the car, we lay packed side by side as the train made its way through Germany. Lice in the straw had already infested our clothing and bodies. While our conditions were deteriorating, we realized we were also in grave danger from Allied air strikes. British and American bombs fell onto the tracks ahead and, over and over again, the train was forced to turn back in an attempt to find an unobstructed route northward. More times than not, train stations were bombed as soon as our transport had pulled out. From the small window, we could see fire around us. Although we were fortunate not to have been directly hit, the trauma was beginning to take its toll.

It was then I began menstruating for the first time. In jail I had only felt shame and ridicule when my mother had sent feminine napkins for my upcoming journey. "See how my mama knew," I whispered to myself. "How wise she was." Now I felt grateful for her foresight. I was thankful we still had our suitcases with us in the car.

The German officers had put one of our fellow prisoners in charge of us. Her name was Jadranka. She was an intelligent and beautiful Croatian woman from Fiume, married to a *carabiniere*. As a teacher in her mid-twenties who spoke German well, she was able to take orders from the German officer. Each time the train changed routes, they routinely took us out for a count, and Jadranka had the responsibility to make sure we were all there. We were warned that if anyone were missing, they would shoot her first and subsequently shoot a group of us in front of the train. It filled us all with fear and kept us from trying anything. We were fortunate that they had recruited a person who did not take advantage of the power the Germans had given her.

The transport train traveled through Germany, seeking a camp that had room for us. It was nearing the end of the war and the camps were all quite full. The train stopped, and the guards removed us from our car to be counted. As I stood in line, I stared at the countryside dotted with fields. A lone farm stood in the distance. A prisoner from my car noticed the sign by the station—"Dresden." She made a connection to the postmark on letters her family had received from her sister, who had been sent away to labor on a farm near a train station with this very name. Claiming her sister worked on that farm, she requested whether the German officer would grant her a visit. We were astonished that, while we were herded back into our car, the officer permitted her to leave. The girl was warned to return within a given amount of time or several of us prisoners would be shot. Although she gave her promise, time seemed to pass slowly as we waited.

The SS again removed us from our car—another count. I feared the girl had fled, or perhaps a different prisoner had escaped. My sense of imminent danger subsided as I observed a figure walking across the distant fields. The young woman was returning. She had kept her promise. Back in the car, she told us all about her sister. We felt encouraged as we heard about the work of picking potatoes on that farm, and especially that the prisoners were fed; no one was starving. It gave us all hope our destination might also be such a place. This girl made it the whole way on the transport. I don't know what happened to her after that. I do know that her sister-in-law, who was also on our transport, later died.

During our time in jail, the newspapers and the nuns' visits had enabled us to keep track of the passage of time, but now, as the days passed, I began to lose my sense of it. Some prisoners took notes of the inhumanity which was beginning to envelop our lives. Among them, Vilmica demonstrated she was as intelligent as she was cute, carefully noting anything she deemed worthy into a journal she carried in her pocket. She told me her father had taught her that one never knows in life what might become useful.

Many others began to lose their struggle to survive. A pregnant woman traveling with her sister-in-law had to urinate frequently. Fortunately, she had a vase that served the purpose. When full, she would empty it out the little window, but one time it bumped one of the window bars and spilled backwards toward her sister-in-law, dousing her in urine. The two women began to quarrel. When our transport arrived in Germany, I noticed they were no longer in our car.

During those days of transport, the SS gave us neither food nor water. However, while still in Austria, through the small window of our cattle car, I saw a group of civilians standing next to the tracks with food in their hands. It seemed strange, as we were not stopped at a station. They handed the food and drink through the bars. It was not much, but I was grateful for the cup of soup I received from these people.

Nonetheless, after only a few days, several prisoners had died due to dehydration, hunger and infection. Those who failed to line up to be counted were routinely removed from the cars. As the days passed, others slowly lost their will to live, and by the time we reached Germany, many more were no longer with us.

If it had not been for the big pan of pork lard with pieces of rind Olga had carried on the transport, perhaps we, too, would

122

have met the same fate. That lard gave our bodies sustenance to withstand the terrible journey and what lay ahead.

Concentration Camps

LOCATIONS OF
CONCENTRATION CAMPS
NAMED IN BOOK

1. Gonars
2. San Sabba
3. Arbe (Rab)
4. Renicci
5. Treviso
6. Neuengamme
7. Bergen-Belsen
8. Ravensbrück
9. Buchenwald
10. Mauthausen
11. Dachau
12. Auschwitz-Birkenau
13. Sachsenhausen
14. Belzec
15. Sobibor
16. Treblinka

MILES
0   200

0   300
KILOMETERS
(approximate)

CHAPTER 13

Survival

It was afternoon when we were finally ordered off the train. We were not at a camp, but in a lovely town lined with store fronts. Carrying our suitcases, we were forced to march through the streets. I wondered what the German civilians must have thought, seeing hundreds of people being paraded through their town. Where did they think we were going? We walked and walked until, at last, we arrived at the imposing entrance gate. Ravensbrück.

As we were moved through the gate, my first look at the scene before me was terrifying. Dead bodies lay strewn on the ground. Many of the prisoners resembled skeletons more than people. I could hear the cries of children coming from the huts. We passed small wagons piled high with corpses. Darkness fell, but we remained standing all night while the SS guarded us, as it was so crowded, there was no room for us in the huts. The only thing we could do was bear silent witness to the ugliness.

125

No age was spared the suffering—the incessant crying of young children from a hut beyond where we stood continued throughout the night. I was struck with the realization that not only was there no way of escape, but likely no future. In the morning, we were marched back through town. We were led through so many places, everything became a blur. The SS guards pushed us onto trucks. Finally loaded back on the train, we were transported to our final destination, Bergen-Belsen.

Through the town of Bergen we were marched. Again I wondered, didn't the townspeople question why we were herded off the packed cars like animals? Couldn't they smell the putrid stench coming from the chimneys of Bergen-Belsen? Trees towered over us as we walked endlessly over the flat, sandy soil.

When we arrived, this camp seemed even uglier than the first. The SS pushed at us roughly, calling us names in guttural German which we could not understand, but whose meaning was clear enough: *"Banditen! Verfluchte Banditen!"* They counted us while they shoved and drove us along, shouting *"Schnell, schnell, achtung!"*

As we approached a building, we quickly opened our suitcases and attempted to put on as much of our clothing as we could. Beginning with three pairs of underpants, we layered on our clothes until we looked all puffed up with the volume of material. We looked so comical that, through our tears, Olga and I weakly laughed at one another. But from inside, the guards had been watching us, and our suitcases were quickly snatched away. At the camp's processing desk, the SS asked us questions: Who could operate a sewing machine? Who was a jeweler by trade? What was your citizenship and date of birth? I was so nervous, I gave them my age instead of my date of birth.

Our frantic dressing in multiple layers turned out to be useless, as the SS allowed us to keep only one of each article of clothing, forcing us to undress in front of them. During this time, they confiscated all our jewelry. I was only wearing cheap costume jewelry, my thin metal bangle bracelets, but they took it all. They even pulled the gold from people's teeth. One partisan woman from Šempas, who later died in the camp, moved quickly to hide her wedding band within her private parts.

Nearby, from her own little corner, a Gypsy[22] stared at me. She appeared unkempt and haggard, yet her eyes were wild with expression. Although I didn't understand her language, I could tell that she wanted my beautiful plaid jacket. With powerful gestures she motioned, "Give me your jacket." But I only held onto it more tightly, as it was so precious to me.

I was wearing a Russian-style fur hat, and I stuck one of my extra pairs of silk stockings into it. One of the *Kapos* saw what I had hidden. She grabbed me by the hair and threw the hat, along with the stockings, onto the huge pile of confiscated personal possessions. As she struck me left and right, I felt the sting of the heavy whip encircle my body, yet the intimidation shook my spirit so greatly, I never noticed the blood dripping from my wounds. We left wearing just one of each article of clothing, not knowing we would eventually lose even those.

As we entered the camp, we stood by an area where a fence separated the male and female prisoners. There was a spigot on the women's side, but it seemed to be out of order. When water flowed intermittently, hundreds of people jostled each other for a chance to drink. A woman filled a bottle with water and threw it over the fence. I stared as the men piled themselves over the container struggling to drink, hands grabbing from one to another, trying to get a drop into their mouths. Few got any. Most of the water spilled onto the ground and the bottle lay there empty.

That first night in the camp, we were pushed into a crowded hut which must have contained a few hundred people. How was it, we wondered aloud, that we could have been delivered to this camp when there was obviously no room for us? Jadranka, our *Kapo*, told us she had overheard the commanding officer saying he had been ordered to deposit us into a camp before he would be allowed to return home.

From inside the filthy hut, we could hear the voices of many different nationalities. Despite the fact that there was clearly not enough room, the guards pushed and shoved us in. We stood there, elbow to elbow, with no room to sit or lie down. Angry at being squeezed more tightly into spaces they had earmarked as their own, a few Gypsy prisoners tried pushing us out again by jabbing us with pins. Every bit of space was precious, for it meant survival.

Unlike so many in our transport car, Olga and I managed to remain together and held tightly to the small comfort we were able to give one another. As night approached, we stood among this unwanted group, prisoners among prisoners, terrified at our circumstances and scared even more of the actions of those determined to guard their territory against us. Finally, overcome by fatigue, we recent arrivals fell asleep on our feet, our exhausted bodies swaying in unison like waves in the darkness.

The second night in the camp, Olga and I decided we would not let ourselves be trapped in that hut again. We slipped through the crowd of prisoners to stand apart from the rest. The clear, moonlit night revealed our surroundings unmistakably: little wagons piled high with corpses, the unremitting crying of children from a nearby hut as we paced through the night, wondering what would become of us. What kind of life could there possibly be in this place, with no room even to sit down? Our weary bodies could not walk forever, back and forth under this star-filled sky. But to enter that hut where we were seen as unwanted threats seemed unthinkable.

As we continued to pace, we witnessed Polish *Kapos* beating their own people who wore the Star of David on their clothes. The men's screams echoed across the fence and through the night.

This was not the idea of camp I had imagined—screams and smoke and burning flesh. To think that Tata and Zora may have been in such a place for so long was unbearable. They must be dead, I realized. They could not possibly have survived. I felt sick with despair for my family, in a way I had not yet grieved for myself.

We wore our own clothes for only a few days until we were again rounded up. *"Achtung, achtung!"* I was shaken at the thought of where they could be taking us.

"Everything off," the *Kapos* ordered. "Line up for the shower." We hung our clothes on hooks along the wall. When we came out of the shower, the SS immediately herded us outside, forcing us to leave our clothing behind, and my beautiful jacket abandoned. I might as well have given it to the Gypsy woman who had wanted it so badly.

We were naked. It was winter, and we shivered from the cold as we passed from that building to another. We were given a number to wear on a tag around our necks and a metal can for eating and drinking, which was tied behind our waists by a string. We were led through a large room filled with sewing machines and piles of fabric and clothing. Striped patches with numbers were being sewn onto the backs of coats, which would identify us as prisoners. Each of us was given one of each article of clothing. I received a long, black dress styled for an old woman, but it was not clean. As I dressed, I felt a sandy scratchiness. These clothes were full of the eggs of lice. We had already seen lice crawling on people around the camp. It immediately became evident we must be wearing the clothes of former prisoners.

When we came out of the barrack, we hardly recognized one another. We were all mismatched. A tall person might be wearing a short dress and a small person a large one. The SS gave no consideration to fit or comfort; they just handed out whatever was on top. I got a coat with the striped patch on the back. It was long to the ankles and black, resembling a man's coat. It was so long, I could hardly walk. Somehow, I was the only one from our group who had managed to hold on to her original shoes. A few days later, a tall woman gestured to ask me whether I would exchange coats with her. Hers was too small and short. I was glad, because it was a beautiful burgundy color and had fur around the neck to keep me warm.

Night after night the SS guards attempted to put the whole group of us into a different hut, but we couldn't fit. Finally, as our numbers began to dwindle, they managed to fit some of us into one hut and others into another. In that way, we eventually lost track of many who had been in our group. They seemed to have simply disappeared, such as the Jewish mother with three daughters who had been on the transport with us. No one knew what had happened to them, and no one wanted to know.

It seemed more than coincidence that Jadranka, our *Kapo* from the transport, also ended up in our hut. Each nationality had its own *Kapo*, and Jadranka was very capable since she spoke Croatian, Italian and German. It occurred to us that perhaps the Germans had ordered her to select a number of us to form a group of a common or related language. Nonetheless, we felt fortunate, because she was different from the other *Kapos* we had seen in the camp. Usually *Kapos* treated their prisoners badly. They were encouraged to keep order by inflicting severe brutality upon their people. The SS guards did not interfere as long as the *Kapos* performed their duty of imposing suffering. By beating their own people, they received more food and privileges. Although Jadranka received extra food rations for giving orders, she was kind to us. She became our friend, and was occasionally beaten because we sometimes did not follow her orders. The SS guards would grab her by her long, red hair, shake her back and forth, and beat her over the head. She asked us to please cooperate with her so she would not get beaten.

By contrast, there was another *Kapo* in our hut from Ljubljana. In a corner of the hut, she had created a small space for herself away from the others. She was husky and strong, and took care of herself by making sure we followed her orders. She was in charge of distributing food, and kept as much as she wanted for herself, doling the rest out as she liked and always giving more to her friends.

There were many different nationalities in our hut. All around us, we heard languages we did not understand. Many had been prisoners for a long time, having arrived on transport from a previous camp. A few had belongings. Next to me there was a Gypsy mother with a daughter who, incredibly, had a small hope chest of possessions, including fine white linens which contrasted sharply with our filthy surroundings. Another prisoner named Sarina was a Jewish girl from Belgrade. She, along with her parents, had been deported to a camp called Auschwitz. Her father did not survive but, after several years of living in that camp, she and her mother were put on an evacuation transport to Bergen-Belsen. I found it comforting that they had managed to remain together for so long, yet it seemed cruel for a mother to have to watch her child suffer through such severe conditions. I suffered as well, now

132

knowing exactly what Tata and Zora had been going through for such a long time, fearing they had not survived. I told myself, "If I were the only one in a German camp, I could be stronger."

Unlike many prisoners who had come before us, we recent arrivals were not in huts with wooden bunks. I had been in several huts, but none of them had bunks. We slept on the dirty, wooden floor stained with fecal matter, since some prisoners could not make it out of the hut in time to relieve themselves. I used my own shoes as a pillow. One morning, one of my shoes disappeared. Someone told me another prisoner had claimed it during the night, so for days I endured walking on the hard, frozen ground with no shoe. Although there was no snow, the cold stung my bare foot. After asking some girls in the hut, one finally revealed she had seen my shoe. Later that day, I felt a small victory to be able to reclaim something of my own.

As new arrivals, we did the bulk of the work and were given the most difficult assignments. We were chosen to dig pits that served as mass graves into which the corpses were thrown. Prisoners who had been in the camp for any length of time were too weak to perform this slave labor. Many did no work at all. They simply sat and stared blankly, seeming barely alive, breathing skeletons who demonstrated little of their former humanity. Having been in these conditions for so long left no hope for the future. They just waited to die, and each day when they lined us up to be counted, many had. Each morning upon awakening, I would find myself near the body of someone who had expired during the night. I remember most vividly a mother who held her baby girl. She had been in the camp for a long time. She held that dead child for days before they noticed. I questioned whether she was even aware her baby was dead.

Every morning the SS, who knew prisoners were dying at a rapid rate, came into the huts and counted us. The dead ones were thrown outside and neatly lined up. Every morning there was a new row of nameless bodies, soon to be discarded to the seemingly endless piles of decaying corpses around the camp.

Whenever we heard the word, *"Achtung,"* we knew we had to line up quickly, or risk a beating. We would stand at attention in the pre-dawn moonlight while the SS, with their guard dog, walked back and forth on the frost-covered ground observing us. We could smell the burning flesh from the nearby crematorium. Every daily line-up instilled fear, for we never knew what they would do to us next. Their sole intent was to inflict suffering, leaving us in a continuous state of terror.

On what must have been a day in March, the SS lined up hundreds of women prisoners and marched us out of the camp. We had no idea where they were leading us. We were first taken to a warehouse, where each of us picked up a burlap sack. We didn't know what was in it, but it was heavy and very full. We walked through the town of Bergen, down tree-lined streets and even past houses. We were already worn out, but we were forced to walk many kilometers carrying that heavy weight over our shoulders. I had so many blisters, I was barely able to walk. The *Kapo* whipped me several times because I couldn't keep up with the others. We took those sacks to the train, which, peculiarly, wasn't located at a station. Instead, it was on tracks in the middle of a field. Soldiers put the bags on the train. We turned around and marched back to camp. We could only speculate about what was in those sacks. By the way in which they were handled, it was clear they must have contained something valuable. I suspected we had just unloaded money, jewels or gold which the SS had seized from fellow prisoners.

One day some girls, who were looking for a relative in the camp, stumbled across a hut the Germans called *Revier*. We had heard this was where they performed experiments on prisoners who could no longer work. Fellow-prisoners had told us they had seen a girl from Vrtojba lying in there. I had to find out whether it was Zora or maybe my distant cousin, Vida, because I knew she had also been sent to Germany. Following their directions, we sneaked to the barrack. There were low windows outside that we were able to peek through. We saw people barely alive lined up on the floor like corpses, with just enough room between them for the staff to walk around. Their bodies, hardly recognizable as human, had endured torture in the name of science, and the presence of medical staff on site made it even more inhumane.

Olga and I began calling out names, although we knew we might not get a response even if she were present. We called each name slowly, repeating it several times. After calling the name, "Vida," we saw a hand slowly begin to rise. She couldn't answer, but with great effort, she was lifting her frail arm.

We knew we were taking a risk as we entered the barrack, but we needed to go to her. When we entered, we saw a corner of the room enclosed by curtains through which we caught a glimpse of medical staff dressed in white. We quickly tiptoed past. Turning toward the area where the hand had gone up, we perused the soon-to-be corpses, hardly recognizing the ruined fragment of what had once been the beautiful red-cheeked girl I had known from my school days, with her blue eyes and natural curly hair. Now Vida lay in the fetal position, with a glass mug by her side containing a little liquid. She couldn't have weighed more than 20 kilos. Her pretty hair was all gone. Remnants of black teeth stuck out between blue, cracked lips. She was barely alive, yet somehow she had heard us call her name. When she saw our faces, it was clear that she recognized us. She reached out and I gave her my hand. Although she seemed to comprehend everything we said, she was too weak to speak. She extended her hand as though she wanted to say, "Tell my mama about me." Her mama didn't know where she had gone, and she was her only daughter.

"Yes, we will tell her," we comforted her. "Don't worry, the end of the war is coming. We've been hearing more and more bombing."

Upon hearing we might soon be free, Vida responded by placing her hands in a praying pose. Her pitiful gesture showed she had understood. We clasped hands once more and gave her our promise. I believe only then Vida was able to die in peace, knowing we would be telling her mama what had happened to her. The following day, I recognized her body on a heap of corpses.

Over the next weeks, we did hear the Allies' continued bombing, and we kept thinking they must be close . . . that maybe we would survive. But after having heard it for such a long time, our hope turned to apathy as the bombing continued. Nothing had changed for us. "We'll remain right here," I thought. "We'll die here."

I was growing progressively weaker, but I knew that if I couldn't work, I might end up in the *Revier*. My teeth were loosening and my gums were swollen with pus. Each day I felt sicker in the stomach. I longed for water, to drink and to rinse my sore mouth, but there was none to be found. During our first weeks in the camp, we had been given coffee each morning and such a thin piece of black bread that we could almost see through it, along with a small pat of margarine. Later, our only sustenance was a soup that resembled dirty water. There was a kind of orange vegetable in it that the prisoners called kohlrabi, along with a few slivers of red cabbage, with pieces of what passed for meat floating on top, so skin-like that they resembled human flesh. Since I was no longer able to chew, and it made me sick to my stomach, I gave my pieces to Olga.

Conditions in the camp were deteriorating rapidly. I felt sicker each day. Many people in our hut had dysentery. Because we slept on the floor in such tight quarters, it was difficult for people to get outside in time to eliminate, and the ground had become contaminated with excrement. It was impossible to clean ourselves unless we could find a piece of clothing from a nearby corpse. Soon Olga and I caught it too.

Next to us was a hut filled with children who had been taken from their mothers upon entering the camp. We often heard their cries at night. I watched as an older child accompanied a younger one out to eliminate—poor little skeletons helping one another. From hut to hut, the epidemic had spread throughout the camp.

I knew if I could not perform labor, my life would be over. As I dug that pit for the dead, I tried to keep my body, heavy from exhaustion, moving to look productive. If they saw me slowing down, I would be whipped. One day I got so desperate for rest that while they counted us, I moved away from our group and escaped to another hut—a hut with people who did not work. I thought I might be able to rest there and they might not notice me. I stayed for one day and one night, but the prisoners, knowing I did not belong, refused to give me any soup.

The next morning, Olga came to find me. It had become obvious to the *Kapos* that several others had also escaped, because the numbers were not correct during their count. She said I needed to return because they had threatened to shoot everyone in the hut if I did not. Reluctantly, I did so, knowing there was no choice but to work until my body gave out completely. I continued to go through the motions, growing weaker each day. Digging. Digging. Feeling so sick. Swallowing the pus that exuded from my aching gums. I had lost all hope I would ever come out alive.

CHAPTER 14

Liberation from Bergen-Belsen, April 15

One day, in the distance across the flat, barren landscape, we suddenly noticed people fleeing. They appeared to be German civilians, families, horses and oxen pulling wagons with their belongings. An incessant parade of people passing through the fields. Escaping? The SS had abandoned the camp, but others took control over us. Some prisoners now seemed to seize the power, ensuring we continued our endless work—digging and digging. In the lookout tower, guards still maintained their posts. Changes were occurring all around us, yet, for us each day remained the same—until the troops arrived. British troops. Trucks. The battalion marching into the camp. I stood at the barbed wire fence and observed the scene.

We went into the huts, telling others the Allies had arrived. We would finally be liberated. Many faces showed no reaction at all to the news. Although they still breathed, no life stirred within them. They did not move, just sat staring blankly, mindlessly. I, too, found it difficult to greet this event with joy, for I knew nothing of what it meant for us. We went back outside to stand and observe. The troops entered the huts to look around, distributing canned beans. After their initial observation, they departed, leaving us feeling abandoned.

After that day, changes did occur. In place of the cruel camp order, chaos ensued. Was the war over? It seemed to be, but we didn't know for sure, and nobody bothered to tell us. The fences that had separated parts of the camp from others were knocked down. Everyone who was still able to move foraged through the camp with a sense of giddiness—skeletons searching to find something, anything to help them survive in this newly created vacuum.

We encountered big storage facilities, rooms filled with supplies. In one building, the first items we found were stacks of sanitary napkins. Even though, due to starvation, we no longer had our periods, we all grabbed as much as we could carry, laughing about the absurdity of taking things for which we had no use. In another building we came across piles of personal belongings, such as clothes, eyeglasses and documents that had been confiscated from the prisoners. There I claimed a colorful plaid cover from a little diary with French writing. The pages had been removed, and I had no idea what purpose it might serve, but it caught my eye and I wanted it. All over the camp, people moved from building to building, taking anything they could find.

One of the first places we went was to the barrack where we had first entered the camp. There, hanging from hooks, were the last sets of clothing the SS had taken from us, hung all in a row. I was ecstatic to find my clothes on the hook exactly where I had placed them. And there was my jacket! I stroked the beautiful red and gold plaid fabric. The happiness of finding it again wiped away, for a brief moment, my suffering. In reclaiming that jacket, I felt I had reclaimed my life.

Although we were liberated, conditions had become even more deplorable. There was no order at Bergen-Belsen. Basic necessities were not yet being met. We were all hungry. Word had spread that the SS had hidden potatoes underground in the camp. Olga found out, and she and others, including the young Gypsy woman from our hut who owned the hope chest, went to search for the buried potatoes. But guards remained in the observation tower and shots were fired. The young woman fell to the ground, dead. After five long years of suffering together, her mother now sat alone in the hut, paralyzed in her grief, gazing in despair at her daughter's fine, white linens, which now—at liberation—represented no future.

When the British returned, they began to demolish the typhus-infested huts. Without the huts, the landscape of Bergen-Belsen had changed, and all across the camp, fires burned brightly. We assisted in the demolition of huts by breaking pieces of wood to cook our potatoes. We foraged for any food we could find. My body longed for vegetables, and we found huge dandelion greens growing among the corpses scattered over the grounds.

One of the storage houses contained ammunition and tents, so we helped ourselves and worked to set up our temporary shelter. We had little idea of how to pitch a tent, but made our best effort. We managed to hook one side of the tent to the barbed wire, but we were unprepared for the April rains that fell right under the tent and left us soaked. We hid our potatoes in our tent under our heads so other prisoners would not steal them. Even though I had slept on them, by morning some potatoes were gone.

British doctors came through the camp and examined us to determine who had contracted typhus. They placed the mark of a 'T' on the foreheads of those infected prisoners. Olga was the first among our friends to fall ill. She lay listless in our tent, unable to even walk. I could tell I was getting sick too.

That night I was overcome by thirst, and I needed to search for water. The moon shone brightly over the camp, exposing the grounds littered with dead bodies. I walked alone, carefully stepping over the decaying remains. Because the fences had been knocked down, I was able to walk far through formerly restricted areas of the camp, so I no longer recognized my surroundings. I must have crossed the line between the men's and women's huts, because I began to see male corpses. I aimlessly entered a deserted hut, where I found a row of spigots. The faucets had been turned on, but not a drop of water ran from them. Beneath, the trough was still filled with water. On the surface of the stagnant water floated scum amidst tiny, floating bubbles, almost glistening from the moonlight flooding in through the nearby door. Thirsty beyond reason, I pushed the floating debris aside and, with cupped hands, quenched my insatiable thirst. Then, I followed my path back to my sick friend.

The British forced the SS to carry the bodies of thousands of dead that had lain on piles or were strewn throughout the camp and lay them out in a respectful manner in order to bury them. The liberated looked on as those who had been their former torturers were now forced to carry out this gruesome task. Vilmica and other friends of ours were interested in observing. They urged me to come along to watch, but by then I, too, wore a 'T' on my forehead. I felt so sick, I was no longer able to do anything. Despondency replaced whatever spirit had remained in me.

Finally, more than a week after liberation, the trucks arrived. The British began moving us from the camp, but first they took us to the building we had entered as new prisoners arriving at Bergen-Belsen. That is where we had first taken off our clothes and experienced the showers. Although I had been in this situation before, this time it felt different. Numbness overtook me. I must have scratched myself, because, as I emerged from the shower, a drop of blood trickled down my leg. An Englishman wanted to medicate me, but I turned to avoid his gaze, for I felt ashamed. Human feelings that had disappeared during those months in Bergen-Belsen were now reappearing as we prepared to reenter civilization. From the showers, we were deloused with DDT to kill the lice that had infested our bodies. Then we boarded the trucks, leaving our contaminated clothes behind to be destroyed. As we drove away, I could only think of my beautiful jacket I had lost again, this time forever.

Late April, 1945

We were taken to an emergency hospital which was set up in the barracks at the Wehrmacht military grounds close to the concentration camp. Olga and I, always together, were given top bunks on the second floor. We were provided with food once a day. At first the nurses checked on us frequently. They removed the sickest and took them downstairs for care. Soon the medical staff was so busy, their rounds became infrequent. Perhaps they did not realize we were so sick, as the marks that had been placed upon our foreheads in the camp had worn off.

When Olga started vomiting, I knew I had to take care of her myself. I ran outside to search for some kind of container for her to use. I walked around the town of Bergen until I came upon an abandoned German helmet lying by the side of the road. Content I had found something to serve as a basin, I found my way back to the barracks. As I tended to Olga, I could feel my own condition worsen. Although I was weak, I could not let her die. We had been through so much together. I had seen where the medical staff nursed the most gravely ill. My only hope was to get Olga there before it was too late, for I realized I would not have the strength much longer to care for her. Feeling dizzy myself, I was barely able to help Olga from her bunk. Leaning her against me, we struggled down the stairs to the room of the critically ill. Bodies close to death filled the room, lying side by side on the floor, waiting to be transferred to the hospital. There were so many sick, they didn't know what to do with her. Upon seeing us, a nurse responded in German that there was no room, but, she added, "If you nail that

144

door shut, you might be able to place her on the floor in front of it."

As she handed me a hammer and some nails, I understood. There were two doors in the room, so I took her advice and hammered nails into the second wooden door until it was securely closed and provided no access into the room. I pulled Olga's listless body in front of it and left her in the nurse's care. I held on tightly to the stair railing as I dragged my exhausted body back up the stairs and crawled into my bunk.

When I tried to get out of bed to go to the bathroom, I jumped from the top bunk, but I was so dizzy, I flew against the door. The impact sent my body tumbling to the floor. I could sense the women in the room staring at me while I lay there, unable to move. The room began to spin, and I thought I would faint. When the blackness passed, I crawled toward my bunk and managed to climb back up. I just lay there motionless. I couldn't get up. I did not try to leave my bed again.

PART II

Out of Delirium

CHAPTER 1

Recuperation

Late May 1945, German military hospital
(In early May, Milena had been transported from emergency
hospital at Wehrmacht barracks to German military hospital.)

After becoming critically ill with typhus, I remembered very little. I did recall having been placed on a conveyor to be deloused. I could not forget the images of body after body, as if on an assembly line, being sprayed with a white powder. I noticed Elvira lying next to me on a stretcher as they placed us side by side into the ambulance. We hadn't seen each other since our days together in the jail cell on Via Barzellini. I don't know whether she recognized me. With balding heads and starved, thin-framed bodies, none of us looked the same. Too weak to acknowledge her presence, I could only listen to the wheels of the truck rolling along the road as we were driven to the German military hospital.

By the time I became fully aware of my surroundings, several weeks had apparently passed. In the German military hospital I occupied a room with other women. The beds were lined up in two rows of three beds each, facing one another. The patients were strangers to me, except for a girl from Šempas named Ana, who I had met in jail and not seen again until now.

For the first time since we had become so very sick at the Wehrmacht barracks, Olga and I were not together. I prayed that she was alive and had been brought here also. We had survived so much together—we needed to leave together. What would I tell her mother if I had to return home without her?

I didn't know how long I had been delirious. Ana and some of the other women in my room told stories of my antics while I had been in my altered state of consciousness. The nurses had referred to me as a challenging patient, always trying to escape. I had been seen running through hospital corridors, causing a disturbance for other patients and trying the patience of the nurses. I remembered that in my lucid moments, I had occasionally found myself groping the walls, feeling my way to a door, "escape" screaming in my head, but I hadn't known where I was or how to accomplish it. Then I would feel myself lifted up and carried back to bed. Some patients had grown weary of my climbing into their beds, and another told of my attempts to uncover her every time I ran free. Now I understood the reason for the nurse who had frequently guarded my bedside.

Friends who visited me during that time never expected me to recover. Through my delirium, I had seen their familiar faces at my bedside. I recalled asking them to go downstairs to ask my mother for some sugar to put in my tea.

As my body slowly grew stronger, I longed only to go home. The doctors, however, refused to discharge me until I was fully recovered. Each time they checked my temperature, I hoped to be well, but I was always disappointed.

"Escape"

Finally, in answer to my prayers, in walked Olga. "I wanted to come sooner," she explained, "but on an earlier visit, Ana told me it wouldn't be worth coming back. You were so sick, Milenka—we all truly thought you would die." I was so glad to see her. We smiled at each other through our tears.

Perhaps because she had gotten sick first, Olga had recovered before me. Already discharged, she had been waiting impatiently for me to get well too, and she had a plan. "Hurry up, let's go!" she said, handing me the clothes she had brought for me. According to the doctors, I was not yet well, but Olga's heart was set on our being together again and away from this place. She helped me dress and, somehow avoiding the medical staff, we quietly rushed through the hospital corridors and fled.

As weak as I still was, stepping out into the fresh air was exhilarating. The seemingly broad street which lay ahead opened a whole new world—a world I had not thought to see again. I swayed from one side of the road to the other, trying to steady myself. The bright yellow forsythia that lined the street

151

signaled the arrival of spring, and it renewed my spirits. I was free. Giddy with happiness, I giggled as I followed Olga on my way back to the Wehrmacht barracks.

The British military had converted the complex of the Wehrmacht barracks to provide provisional housing for the liberated prisoners. We were each given a bed, a few articles of clothing, and our own dish. Mine was white ceramic with a delicate print around the rim, and the daily meals I ate from it nourished my body. Gradually, I felt myself getting stronger.

Convalescent Villa in Osterwald, Germany

After several weeks, our accommodations for convalescence had been arranged, and, because Olga had sprung me from the hospital, we were able to remain together. Many of the girls I had met in the camp were sent to other locations in Germany, so, unfortunately, we lost contact with one another. When the trucks arrived to take us "displaced persons" to various sites, Olga and I could not risk being separated again. We stood side by side as we hopped up into the truck, anticipating where this next trip would take us.

Olga and I ended up in the village of Osterwald, in a villa housed with German workers obliged to give hospitality to concentration camp survivors who needed convalescence. Osterwald, about thirty kilometers south of Hanover, was a nice village with a church. We were happy that our *Kapo*, Jadranka, and Sarina, another friend from our hut at Bergen-Belsen, were in our villa too. That made us a group of four companions. Sarina's mother and cousin were also housed with us, making a total of about fifteen women, most of whom were Croatian and Serbian.

In our villa, it was as though we were a family. The "father" of our house made the rules which we were expected to obey, and German people served us until we recuperated. Although typhus had left us thin and still losing our hair, we enjoyed our time there. They took care of us. They fed us. From our beds, we could request an egg or something else to eat. This, along with the constant thought of returning home, gave me the strength I needed to regain my health.

Figure 13. Milena and friends in Osterwald, Germany after their recuperation from Bergen-Belsen. Behind from left to right, Jadranka, Olga, and Sarina, with Milena lying in front (1945)

After we fully recovered, the four of us had fun. Olga, Jadranka, Sarina and I went out together. I had become a young woman and, after what we had endured, it felt so good to be alive. The British troops were a constant presence in the area. Soldiers often visited us, giving us chocolates and taking photos of us together. One time we disobeyed the house rules and hitchhiked on British trucks. We ended up at the port of Hamburg, where the soldiers invited us onto their ship. While we sipped tea and nibbled at sweets, we tried to engage in conversation. Neither Olga nor I spoke English, but we were able to communicate with some words in German. Jadranka was older and more educated, so she did most of the talking. At the end of the evening, the soldiers drove us back home, but our "father" found out, and we were punished and not permitted to go out for a week. It had been worth it.

Male camp survivors often traveled around to the different villas to visit people of their own nationality. That was how we met Bojan, a Slovenian man of approximately fifty years of age. He befriended us, and we enjoyed being in the company of such a kind, older person who spoke our language. One day he surprised each of us with a gift—mine was a beautiful pair of gray sandals with heels. He hadn't even asked my size, but they fit perfectly. We didn't know where he would have gotten the money, but we never questioned his generosity. I had lost all my own clothes. The Red Cross had given me a few articles of clothing, but now I owned something that really belonged to me. I wore my elegant sandals with pride.

We always looked forward to having guests at the villa who spoke our mother tongue, so we especially enjoyed the day a group of young Slovenian and Croatian men, also liberated from

Bergen-Belsen, visited us. It was comforting to share stories and exchange ideas in our native language, and we simply had fun in the company of others our own age. However, we did not expect our pleasant time to end so abruptly.

As Olga and I were standing by a wall outside in the yard of the villa, a truck pulled up. It stopped suddenly in front of the house and out jumped a group of young German civilians. There must have been ten to fifteen men. Some pulled out whips from their pants. Others flew toward us swinging clubs. They attacked our male guests, beating them with their weapons and slashing their bodies with the too familiar sound of the whip. We expected to be beaten as well, but they left as quickly as they had arrived.

As the truck sped off in a trail of dust, I realized that even though the war was over, much of the hatred persisted. The Germans would not give us peace. German youth groups had not been dismantled, and they continued to propagate the ideas of Nazi Germany.

Because Olga and I were the only ones who had seen the whole attack, we volunteered to testify. Alone, we probably would have declined, but together we felt more courageous. It was only right that we provide evidence for these men, who had suffered yet another injustice.

* * * *

Traveling with soldiers in a British army tank, we headed toward Hanover to the British headquarters. As we stood in front of the small tank window slit, we saw destruction all around us. Buildings were in ruins from the Allied bombing. Many roads had become impassable. On both sides, rubble was piled high. The tank continued on through, creating its own path where nothing else could pass. Olga and I felt important traveling with our liberators as we headed across war-torn Germany.

CHAPTER 2

Returning Home

As the time for us to go home approached, all of us in the villa were preoccupied. Finally, Sarina's cousin expressed what no one had yet spoken aloud: "I don't want to go home. I'm afraid to go home . . . afraid to find no one."

My worries were the same. After what I had lived through in Bergen-Belsen, I knew Tata and Zora could not have survived more than a few months under similar conditions. I was sure Pepe had been killed, and it was possible that the rest of my brothers were dead as well. It was my hope that Vilma and Silva had remained home with Mama and Lučano, but after the destruction I had witnessed, I couldn't help but wonder if my home would still be standing.

It was September grape season when Olga and I finally began the long train journey home. Dressed in shorts we had sewn ourselves, Olga and I sat in the open boxcar as it made its way south across Germany. I remembered how, on our way to

Bergen-Belsen, station after station had been bombed the very moment our transport had pulled away. During the war, the Nazis had forced crews of inmates from the camps to maintain the tracks so supplies and transports could reach Germany. I now understood how dispensable they had considered the lives of those prisoners.

The Allies had bombed the German rail system extensively during the war. During much of our journey home, we passed workers, though no longer prisoners, repairing the broken system. Occasionally our train passed over temporary bridges spanning fast-flowing rivers far below. With feet dangling over the edge of the boxcar, wide-eyed, we peered down at the perilous depths.

We didn't know the exact route we had been traveling, but we became aware of our location when our train stopped in Austria. We spent the night in meager accommodations, along with many others who were returning home. The air was heavy with anticipation, and all around we could hear *Lager* (concentration camp) survivors asking each other if they had seen one of their parents, siblings, even their children in a camp.

Our final destination was Postumia, Italy (Postojna in Slovene). From there, we had to find our own way home. Many, including our friends Jadranka and Sarina, traveled on to Croatia and Serbia. As Olga and I jumped off the train in Postojna, we recognized a partisan from our hometown of Vrtojba. "Do you know anything about our families?" we called out.

"Slauko is dead," he revealed to Olga. "The war was almost over when his cannon went off while he was cleaning it."

"Has my father come home yet?" I impatiently asked.

"No," he replied, "and neither has your sister."

"And my brother Pepe?"

"He was executed."

Pepe's death was not a surprise, but my hopes for Tata and Zora were suddenly destroyed.

The final leg of our journey was filled with trepidation—the fear of learning more bad news. We found our way around the city to a piazza, where a vegetable market had been set up. A vegetable truck from our area was departing Postojna for its return trip, and the driver offered us a ride. We didn't hesitate to jump on the back, and the truck took us all the way to Gorizia.

By the time we were dropped off at the park on Corso Verdi, it was nighttime. There was an early fall chill in the air. We sat down on a bench facing the street to deliberate how we would get home to Vrtojba in the dark. Moments later, two boys passing by on bicycle, noticing our condition, called out to us, "Where have you been?"

"In a *Lager* in Germany." we answered.

They offered us a ride home on their bikes. They wanted to take us all the way to Čuklje Street, but we told them to drop us off on the main road of town, as we didn't want them to know exactly where we lived. Olga's aunt's house was the first we passed, but she wasn't at home, so Olga ran next door to Yelko's family's *osteria* to look for her. She wasn't there either, but Yelko was. The first words out of his mouth were, *"Je prišla tudi Milenka?"* ("Has Milenka come too?")

"She's outside," Olga replied. He was probably too embarrassed to step out immediately since he was surrounded by family, and I was too impatient to linger. My only thought was getting home to Mama.

I walked the short distance down the Čuklje with cautious anticipation. A small bag slung over my shoulder carried all my possessions—a metal *Lager* ID tag, the cover of a prisoner's diary and the white ceramic dish from which I had eaten during my recovery at the Wehrmacht barracks. Some clothes received from the Red Cross padded my bag.

It must have been ten o'clock by the time I walked through the gate to my house. In the darkness, I opened the door. Mama stood alone in the kitchen, mouth hung open in shock. It was clear she had never expected to see me again. Her pale blue eyes welled with tears. *"Oh! Ubogi otrok, si prišel domov,"* she cried. ("Oh! Poor child, you've come home.")

There were no more words to say. Mama and I embraced, and for the first time, I shed the tears which I could not have cried in Germany. For a brief moment, I forgot about the sadness. I was home at last, and nothing could change that.

I could have remained in Mama's arms forever, but into the house walked Yelko, to see whether what Olga had told him was really true. Happy to see him, but even happier to be back, I flitted around the house, taking in the reality that I was finally home, my house was intact, and the war was over.

A few days after Olga and I had come home, we delivered the news to Mama's cousin about her daughter, Vida. Only we knew her fate, how she had spent her last days, and now we had to fulfill her dying wish. It was so difficult to tell her mother her only daughter was gone. Her mama's quiet sadness seemed to confirm her innermost thoughts. She must have gone straight to church, for within an hour we heard the bells from the steeple tower ringing across Vrtojba.

About a week later, we heard shots coming from down the street. I ran to the gate to see a male figure coming down the Čuklje, rifle in hand, joyfully shooting into the air as though to announce his homecoming. It was my brother Milan. Years had passed since we had last seen one another. He stared ahead as though he didn't recognize me, for I had been just a skinny child when he had left for the military. As he approached the gate, his gaze showed his disbelief that before him stood a grown sister. We just stared at one another. He dropped his rifle and we hugged, squeezing each other tightly. Milan knew nothing about Pepe, Tata or Zora, but for the moment, his safe return was all that mattered.

CHAPTER 3

Discoveries

In the months following my return, families all over Vrtojba experienced both happiness and heartache. Doors of countless homes opened to find loved ones who had been assumed dead. For other families, the door never opened, and the tragic reality of a loved one never returning had to be faced. Although we, too, were beginning to face the inevitable, we prayed that, by some miracle, Tata and Zora would return to us.

As more survivors returned from Germany, rumors spread about acquaintances they had seen in the camps. One of Tata's cousins in Austria wrote a letter telling us she had received a message that Tata had been in Dachau. We couldn't imagine how Tata had managed to get a message outside of the camp, but this communication gave us hope. Tata's last words had been that he would be back. How I longed to believe them. Days later, a fellow prisoner informed us that he and Tata had been sent to Neuengamme, where they had worked in a swampy area. We were relieved to learn Tata had still had the strength to work.

We had heard nothing, however, about Zora, who had been gone for a year now. She, too, I felt, was dead. I remembered the many people who had accompanied me on the transport to Germany, but how so few of them had survived Bergen-Belsen.

I had been home for more than a month and had nearly given up hope of seeing my sister again. Yet, against all odds, she too walked through the front door. Unlike me, Zora emerged with several suitcases filled with beautiful clothing, jewelry, and even an umbrella. Her Russian liberators had looted German homes, and she had become the lucky recipient. "Do you like those boots?" the soldiers had asked her.

"Yes."

"Then take them off," they had ordered the young German woman.

I was jealous of her beautiful silk dresses and brooches. I owned a single dress that I had received when the Red Cross distributed used clothes, while Zora wore a different dress every time she went out dancing. She was so pretty and adorned in such finery, that she had many suitors calling on her.

In spite of Zora's extensive wardrobe, just as I, she had suffered greatly. She had been in the concentration camp of Auschwitz, and she showed me the identification number permanently tattooed on her forearm. "I never thought I'd survive," Zora shared. "I was so hungry I once stole some garbage, and the SS practically beat me to death. Another time I had been with a group of prisoners on my way to the gas chamber. I couldn't believe it when a *Kapo* pulled me out of line at the last moment."

Zora told me about a young woman from a nearby town who tried to end her life by touching the electric barbed wire surrounding the camp. "Somehow I was able to stop her that day, but weeks later I found myself considering that same alternative to endless torture."

As the Russian troops had drawn nearer, the Germans had evacuated most of the Auschwitz prisoners from the camp. Zora, along with many other prisoners, had been placed on a transport which ended up near Berlin, where she performed slave labor in a German airplane factory.

In May, when the Russian military liberated Berlin, she and some other fellow prisoners faced further suffering. She was one of the few women not infested with lice. "For some unknown reason, the lice didn't like me," Zora explained. "But it proved to be a curse," she went on, "for when some of the Russian soldiers became drunk and wanted sex, they considered me more desirable." Zora managed to evade their pursuit by hiding in the hay, but the sexual violence committed against many other female survivors made liberation a continuation of torture. Zora took me to visit a friend from Bilje who had accompanied her home from Germany. A concentration camp survivor, she lay dying in bed, a victim at the hands of the Nazis, as well as her Russian liberators.

During those months, we gradually learned about the fate of many friends and acquaintances across Vrtojba. There was a rumor that Jožef Gorkič, the friend Tata had accompanied on the night he was caught, had escaped from his transport to Germany. Since he never returned home, we concluded that he probably died in Germany. New information caused us to blame him for Tata's capture—he had been working for both sides, the fascists and the partisans. In that way he had been able to obtain passes from both and was always ready to pull out the appropriate pass when questioned, eluding capture until that night. Gorkič knew whether the fascists or Germans had been in that area. That is why he had given the partisan pass for Tata to hide in his hat. Our father had been too helpful and trusting.

We continued to wait for Tata's return. His brother Guštek, who lived in Ljubljana, had also been deported to Dachau. We learned he returned home from Germany, but had not seen Tata while he was in Dachau. I thought that perhaps Tata could still be recovering in Germany. Many survivors in the villas had been too weak to return home when I had. But then someone from Bilje reported he had seen Tata on a stretcher near the end of the war, barely able to speak. He witnessed Tata handing his meager ration of margarine to a young prisoner nearby. He must have known the food would have been of greater value to a healthier prisoner. The letter from the Red Cross confirming Tata's death did finally arrive. He had been in several *Lagers*, including Dachau, and had been transferred to Neuengamme where he eventually died.

I was not surprised to learn Pepe had been executed in the mountains of Lokve. I believed I had had a premonition while in the hospital. The Decima Mas had caught him on the bridge doing patrol, fully armed. He was alone. Vilko had often guarded that bridge. But on that night Vilko had asked Pepe to do it. We learned that Vilko had been a spy, working on both the fascist and partisan sides. He had been aware the fascists were nearby and had purposefully placed Pepe's life in danger.

Even Vilko's father had been shrewd. We now realized how he had sometimes traveled to different towns during the war years without putting his life in jeopardy. Just as Vilko, he had obtained passes from both the partisans and the fascists. Nevertheless, Vilko's treason did not go unpunished. After the war, he was jailed by the partisans.

Vilma told me that at the end of the war, before Zora and I had returned, Vilko had boldly come to our home and, claiming his innocence, had begged her in vain to testify on his behalf. After Zora returned from Germany and learned the truth about Vilko, her tumultuous rage resounded throughout the house. "He was sending me everywhere, and I did everything he asked me to do, delivering messages, maybe even against me and my family!" she screamed.

Now it had become clear why Vilko had not wanted her to go home on bicycle through the town of Bilje the evening she was caught. As a spy, he had known about the *rastrellamento*. It was inconceivable that this was the same man who had been a source of such happiness for Zora. Vilko had been responsible for so much of our family's suffering, made all the more unthinkable because it had come at the hands of a friend.

CHAPTER 4

The Funeral

It was November before the families were able to make the journey to Lokve, where Pepe had been executed, to reclaim the remains of their sons. Stanko accompanied Mama on the bus into the mountains. Guided by the lone survivor of those twenty partisans, they followed the treacherous road winding its way upward toward the snow-topped peaks to the pit where nineteen partisans lay.

Where had the partisan troops been on that April day? They had been fighting in the area. Why hadn't they attacked the Germans? These were the questions that these families from all over northern Italy asked themselves as they neared the site.

The surviving partisan from Tolmino led the way through the woods to find his comrades. Without his assistance, we would have never known where the bodies lay. Meanwhile, Stanko stopped at the home of a nearby farmer to warm up and bring a hot drink for Mama. Loved ones waited in the cold for the search party to recover the remains.

The German executioners had separated the twenty partisans into two groups of ten, each facing a natural forest pit with a diameter of about four meters. The men who had fallen into the bottom of the pit lay intact. Some of the bodies were no longer recognizable, for the forest was home to wildlife, including wolves. Pepe's remains, being found on top, was one of those. His corpse, little more than bones, was one of the last to be carried out. Amid the decomposition, Mama detected a small swatch of blue striped fabric. She identified it as material from a shirt she had made for Pepe. She examined the teeth, and knew she had finally found her son. One father from Milano scrutinized the remains to distinguish his son's skeleton from the others. In vain, he decided to simply take one body home, pronouncing, "Our children have been comrades in life, have suffered together and now lay together in death, so one is as good as any other."

* * * *

The funeral service was held in Piazza Vittoria, the notable square in the center of Gorizia. Posters had been hung around the city and the suburban towns notifying the public of the somber occasion. On November 25th, one hundred and twelve partisans who had been found in the surrounding mountains, including the bodies of Pepe and his comrades, were eulogized. At the foot of the baroque Church of Sant' Ignazio, rows of coffins spread across the piazza. It was a huge funeral, and people from all over Gorizia and neighboring towns came to mourn. Olga's family was present for her brother Slauko. Some, simply onlookers, had arrived to hear firsthand the somewhat legendary story of these twenty partisans. In spite of our loss, we felt fortunate so many in our family had survived. Many families had suffered even greater losses.

Travnik v Gorici, 25. novembra 1945; pogreb 112 padlih partizanov.
Piazza Vittoria a Gorizia, 25 novembre 1945: funerale di 112 partigiani caduti

Figure 14. The funeral for 112 partisans on November 25, 1945
Courtesy of Isonzo Soča, Giornale de Frontiera (Foto: Altran)

I thought about Pepe's last words to Lučano: "I'm fighting for you, not for myself. For me it's too late." I remembered the last time I saw Pepe alive in the courtyard of the jail. He had whispered, "I won't be going to Germany." Now I knew what he had meant. He had already understood his fate.

In unadorned black dresses received through the Red Cross, we listened intently as the survivor from Tolmino began his speech—the whole story of what happened on the day Pepe was killed. These were his words as we remembered them:

> "It was April 4, nearly the end of the war, when our usefulness to the enemy was over. We had always suspected we would be killed. On a truck, the Germans took us twenty partisans up into the mountains to Lokve. In the forest, we had to chop down big trees all day long. As they watched us work, the Germans stood around eating food from tin cans. They made us carry those heavy logs while they beat us. When evening arrived, weak and disheartened, we were lined up facing a pit—two groups of ten, staring at the shrubbed abyss. Knowing there was little chance of escape but understanding I had nothing to lose, I turned and began praying in order to distract them. I begged the Germans, with weapons in hand, to have mercy for the sake of my elderly mother. I pleaded with them to spare me for her. Then, leaping into the shrubs below, I ran. They shot after me, but the bullets only grazed my skin. As I ran, I heard the shots and screams of my comrades. They wasted no time, for they didn't want anyone else to escape. I ran and ran as far as I could. Then I hid in the brush, quietly waiting for it to be over. A farmer in the area later reported he had heard

the shots and screams echoing from the woods.
I waited and waited until it was quiet."

All across the piazza, the mass of mourners stood in silence, bearing witness to the last moments in the lives of their sons, nineteen comrades who had stood side by side as they met their death. I glanced around at the crowd praying quietly, weeping and staring at the nineteen caskets lined up, side by side among the other fallen soldiers.

At this funeral, I could not cry. Somehow, I felt I had already witnessed Pepe's funeral from my hospital bed. In a way, I had already grieved. I had no more tears to shed. Perhaps I'd seen too much misery, too many dead.

The wooden coffins were carried to the awaiting horse-drawn wagons to begin the journeys to their resting places in their respective towns. Coffins going to Vrtojba were placed on the farmer's wagon, and we followed our procession as it went from Piazza Vittoria to Via Oberdan—on to Corso Verdi, turning left onto Via XXIV Maggio, past the stately *tribunale* toward the town of Šempeter. We followed. The horses' hooves clopped along the road, all the way to Vrtojba.

Pepe was coming home. Except for Tata, our *"famiglia numerosa"* was together once again. We had survived the war.

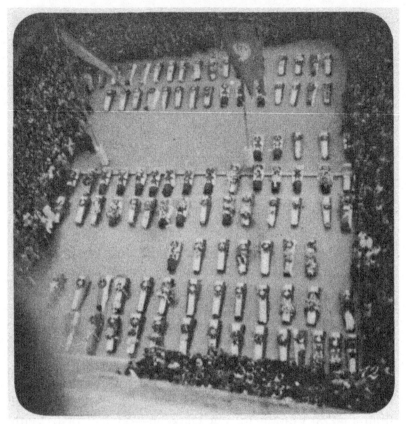

Figure 15. A view of the coffins in Piazza Vittoria from above
Courtesy of Isonzo Soča, Giornale de Frontiera (Foto: Altran)

November 1, 2008
(63 Years Later)

On this Day of the Dead, Olga and I found ourselves at the cemetery in Vrtojba adorning the graves of loved ones. We've seen each other infrequently over the years, as she has lived in Vrtojba, and I have spent the last forty years in Gorizia, since moving back from the United States.

The passing of time has taken its toll on us, our bodies moving a bit more slowly. Olga has health concerns, and I have had recent hip surgery. For a brief moment, I see us as girls, climbing cherry trees in the orchards of Vrtojba, dressed in the identical dresses Lucija had made for us.

Olga and I had gone through so much together, yet our painful war memories had remained unspoken, unshared for more than sixty years. I had locked mine away in a separate part of my being, as though their mere mention might conjure up the horrors themselves—horrors I never wanted to relive.

Happy to see one another, we shared our news of children, grandchildren and the birth of my first great-grandchild. A pause in the conversation gave me the opportunity to boldly ask her what, for so many years, I had wondered: "Olga, do you remember in Germany when I found you that helmet to throw up in?"

Olga remained silent for a long moment, staring straight ahead at the plots where our brothers, Pepe and Slauko, were laid to rest. "I remember. And do you remember, Milenka," she continued, "when I picked you up at the hospital?"

"I remember," I whispered.

Figure 16. Olga and Milena (2013)

PART III

The War's Aftermath:
Consequences for Milena, Her Family
and the Border Region

CHAPTER 1

Repercussions of War on a Region
and Its People

On May 1, 1945, while Milena was recovering in Germany, Tito's Partisan Resistance forces, which had fought along with the Allies, liberated the areas of Trieste and Gorizia from German occupation. Allied British troops entered Trieste the following day and forced the surrender of any remaining German forces. Although control of the area eventually was to be decided through the Paris Peace Conference, a provisional government was set up by the Yugoslav partisans. Most Italians, historically prejudiced against the Slavs, were hostile to this occupation. They feared revenge, as well as the possibility they could lose this northeastern corner of Italy to future Communist Yugoslavia. However, for most of the Slovenes in the area around Gorizia, the arrival of the communist partisans was considered freedom from the terror of their Nazi occupiers, as well as liberty from the oppression of fascism.

During the forty days of partisan occupation, thousands of civilians, military personnel and officials, especially Italians in the area of Gorizia and Trieste, were arrested. Many were deported to detention camps, and some were subsequently executed and thrown into geological chasms known as *foibe*. Located in the limestone plateau region around Trieste and into Istria, known as the Carso (Italian), Kras (Slovene) or Karst (German), these *foibe* are cavernous pits with narrow openings on the surface, and, in some cases, a few hundred meters deep.

Controversy continues to surround the *foibe* deaths. Although some on the political Right tend to exaggerate the number of victims, notable regional historians have more or less agreed upon the numbers. Native Slovene Bogdan C. Novak, a professor of European history who lived in the zone during the time of the border conflict, wrote, "According to Italian statistics, the communists arrested about 6,000 persons in the Trieste and Gorizia areas. Of these about 1,850 were deported, out of which about 1,150 never returned and are presumed to be dead."[23] Italian historians Galliano Fogar and Raoul Pupo count the number of those who never returned as between 1,000 and 1,800 Italian, as well as anti-communist Slovenian victims. These numbers also correspond closely to "[t]he Red Cross estimates that 2,250 failed to return."[24]

Ignoring and even forgetting the violence against the Slovenes and Croatians during fascism and World War II, there are those on the Italian Right who consider the *foibe* killings simply as terrorism or ethnic cleansing against innocent Italians. Right-wing politicians from 1945 to the present have often used the *foibe* executions to exemplify Slavic "barbarism" and perpetuate prejudice against the Slovenian people. In contrast, immediately after the war, the Yugoslav partisans felt justified to arrest and execute anyone associated with the Fascist regime as retribution for atrocities to the Slovenes and Croatians over a period of twenty years. Moreover, they wanted to dispose of anyone, even Slovenes and anti-fascists, who opposed their plan to incorporate Gorizia and Trieste into a communist-ruled Yugoslavia. Unfortunately, during this operation, their plan of action became unbridled, and a number of innocent people were among the victims.

Figure 17. Procession of demonstrators and partisans during the "forty days" of the Yugoslav administration of Gorizia from May to June, 1945
Courtesy of *Isonzo Soča, Giornale di Frontiera*

Figure 18. Trgovski Dom, and later, Casa del Popolo, during the Allied Military Government occupation, 1946.

The Allied Military Government (AMG) took over in June 1945, replacing the provisional government of the Yugoslav partisans. The approximate area of the Adriatic Littoral was soon divided into two zones by a temporary boundary called the Morgan Line. Zone A, which included Trieste, Gorizia and its suburban towns within the province, such as Šempeter and Vrtojba, was controlled by the AMG. The Military Government of the Yugoslav Army controlled Zone B, which included the area south of Trieste, extending into Istria. The region became a "political hot spot." By November, the American Blue Devil 88th Army Division occupied Gorizia and vicinity in order to maintain peace between the Italians and the Slovenes.[25] Due to the advent of the Cold War, the AMG feared Communist Yugoslavia and, therefore, used Italian authority to administer the city. For this reason, Slovenes continued to suffer some injustices even under the American occupation.

In Gorizia, neither the Italians nor the Slovenes wanted to lose their city, the cultural and commercial center of the area. While the Allies of the Soviet Union, France, Great Britain and the United States deliberated on a permanent border solution, demonstrations erupted on city streets in Gorizia. Those who wanted Gorizia to become part of Yugoslavia sometimes carried or displayed Yugoslav flags, shouting, *"Hočemo Gorica"* or "We want Gorizia." Although demonstrations were generally peaceful, American Military Police (MP) sometimes used force to control the situation. Jeeps drove through the streets and often on the sidewalks in an attempt to keep civilians at home. With hoses, they sprayed pedestrians to keep them off the streets of the city. Occasionally, unsuspecting people were injured while they did nothing more than walk home from work.

Milena described some anecdotal evidence of this force. "A girl from Vrtojba was injured when returning home from work one such day. Walking down the sidewalk near the *tribunale* on her way, the MPs suddenly came from behind in their jeep and ran her down. On another occasion following our return from Germany, Zora and I attended a Slovenian meeting at *Casa del Popolo*, formerly called *Trgovski Dom*. Afterwards, we rode our bicycles down Corso Verdi, turning the corner at Via Garibaldi, when suddenly an Italian man and woman came running toward us. He grabbed the handlebars of my bike to bring it to a stop, while she slapped my face. At that moment, an American army truck drove down the street and, witnessing a disturbance, the MPs were quick to capture me. Fortunately, a friend of Vilma's, who was affiliated with the AMG, recognized me and came to my defense.

My brother Stanko was less fortunate. During a peaceful demonstration near the park, he was grabbed by the MPs and thrown into their truck. He spent time in jail, and I later attended the trial, where he was found innocent."

Figure 19. Demonstration in Gorizia's Piazza Vittoria, in the last months before the Paris Peace Treaty was signed. Those on the left with Yugoslav flags wanted the city to be incorporated into Yugoslavia, while others insisted that Gorizia remain in Italy. Courtesy of Musei Provinciali, Gorizia

Border decisions (Map illustration xii)

On February 10, 1947, the Paris Peace Treaty was signed. It defined the permanent border between the Republic of Italy and the Yugoslav Federal People's Republic, which went into effect on September 15. It was decided that Zone B would go to Yugoslavia. Trieste became a Free City until 1954, when it was transferred back to Italy. Most of Zone A, including Gorizia, went to Italy, leaving the suburban towns without their city.

This meant that Milena's family and others in those small towns and rural areas who had been residents of the province of Gorizia, Italian citizens for more than twenty years, would now live in Yugoslavia. Slovenes in towns such as Vrtojba, Bilje and Šempeter had thought it impossible that the city of Gorizia would be awarded to Italy, especially since Gorizia had been liberated by the Yugoslav troops. Most devastating was that these people would lose their city, and would now live in an area isolated from any municipal center. Gorizia had been their county seat, as well as the commercial and cultural hub. Farmers had come daily with carts of goods to earn a living, people held jobs, and the city had been their only source for shopping and entertainment. It simply didn't seem fair.

This change resulted in an immediate migration of people from one side of the border to the other. Most Italians living in the area which now belonged to Yugoslavia packed up and moved to the Italian side. Some Slovenes in Gorizia, possessed with a nationalist spirit or who wished to be part of the new hope of socialism, migrated several blocks east across the border to Yugoslavia. One Italian aristocrat living on the border managed to persuade those drawing the line to include her house on the Italian side. However, most people simply stayed put and allowed the new political border to divide them.

In September of 1947, days before the border was finalized, Milena remained on the Italian side in order to marry a corporal she had met in the American Blue Devil 88th Army Division. Because she moved to the United States, she never began a new life in Yugoslavia with her family in Vrtojba, nor did she witness the dramatic changes that later occurred on this border.

Figure 20. Soldiers of the American Blue Devil 88th Army Division mark the border dividing Italy and Yugoslavia.
Courtesy of *Isonzo Soča, Giornale de Frontiera (Foto: Altran)*

Figure 21. This square, with its Transalpina train station, was divided between the two countries, with the station on the Yugoslav side. Barbed wire would eventually block the passage of people and merchandise from one side to the other. (1947) Courtesy of *Isonzo Soča, Giornale di Frontiera*

At the train station that had once been in Gorizia, the "iron curtain" division between the communist world of Eastern Europe and the anti-communist West became a point where people, now separated by barbed wire and guards, might catch a glimpse of their relatives on the other side. On the roof of the station, facing Italy, stood a red star. Beneath it were the words, "*Mi Gradimo Socializem,*" or "We are Building Socialism."[26]

The Slovenian population who remained on the Italian side organized its own societies and schools soon after the war. However, the issue of minority rights was not addressed by Italy until the Law on the Protection of the Slovenian Minority was finally passed by Parliament in 2001.[27]

The building of a city

Only meters away, in a meadow on the Yugoslav side, grew the dream to design and construct a new urban center. These new residents of Yugoslavia who had lost Gorizia didn't know where or how to begin building a town. One resident voiced, "It was like entering a dark tunnel. There was nothing here. I had lived in a town where Italian was spoken and had never had any education in Slovenian."[28]

The Central Committee of the Party of Belgrade decided the Federation would finance the building of Nova Gorica, or "New Gorizia." Volunteer work brigades soon arrived from all over Yugoslavia, and the fields and vineyards were filled with approximately six hundred youth, armed with shovels, picks and wheelbarrows, speaking several different Slavic languages, laboring intensively to build a city. With determination and robust enthusiasm, they began with a wide road and constructed buildings around it. By the early 1950s, the residents of Nova Gorica had the essential structures to function as a town.[29]

More than sixty years later, Nova Gorica is a bustling, modern urban center. With a town population of 15,000, it serves as the municipal seat for a population of approximately 32,000 in the area. Slovenia, a democratic republic, gained its independence from Yugoslavia in 1991. In 2004, it joined the European Union. In a Europe without borders, Gorizia and

Nova Gorica remain connected by roads that lead Italians and
Slovenes to appreciate each city for its unique character.
(See map illustration xiii.)

Figure 22. This 1928 view shows the valley where the future Nova Gorica would be
built. Due to heavy WWI bombing, the mountains stand treeless, and the destroyed
cemetery was eventually moved to a new site. At the foot of the mountain lies the
town of Solkan.
Courtesy of *Isonzo Soča, Giornale di Frontiera*

Figure 23. Cemetery gone, this site, photographed during WWII, would become the location of Nova Gorica.
Courtesy of *Isonzo Soča, Giornale di Frontiera*

Figure 24. The same site, with the small, but growing city of Nova Gorica, 1970
Courtesy of *Isonzo Soča, Giornale di Frontiera* (Foto: Goriški Muzej, Slovenia)

190

Figure 25. With shovels and picks, youth from volunteer organizations all over Yugoslavia arrive to help construct the new city of Nova Gorica.
Courtesy of *Isonzo Soča, Giornale di Frontiera* (Foto: Goriški Muzej, Slovenia)

Figure 26. Taking a gymnastics break during the building of the city. The words on the roof of the building behind reads, "Death to Fascists."
Courtesy of *Isonzo Soča, Giornale di Frontiera* (Foto: Goriški Muzej, Slovenia)

Figure 27. Marshall Tito giving a speech near the border about the city of Trieste and the border issue in early 1950s.
Courtesy of *Isonzo Soča, Giornale di Frontiera* (Foto: Goriški Muzej, Slovenia)

Figure 28. (View of Yugoslav hill from Gorizia) To commemorate Marshall Tito, *Naš Tito* (Our Tito) was carved into the mountain by the Yugoslav Army in the 1970s.
Courtesy of *Isonzo Soča, Giornale di Frontiera*

The shared experience of Bergen-Belsen

After the end of the war and her return home, Milena lost contact with many of the young women she had met in jail and in Bergen-Belsen. Many, such as Jožica, never returned. As far as she knew, Sarina and her mother had found their way home to Belgrade. Vilmica and Elvira returned home to Gorizia. Shortly after the war, Jadranka did correspond with Milena and Olga. Because the Nazis had selected her to act as *Kapo* at Bergen-Belsen, her life was later threatened by the partisans. She requested that Olga and Milena write a letter as testimony that she had been kind to the people in her charge. Indeed, she had, for they recalled the numerous times the SS had beaten her when she had been too sympathetic toward them. Aside from communicating such essential information, these survivors had seldom discussed the terrible events of the past with one another. After the war was over, they simply wanted to go on with their lives.

In recent years, Milena has occasionally communicated with Vilmica and Olga about their shared past, poignant memories from a time and place only they could understand. During their conversations, they have even given each other new information on the events they had experienced seventy years ago.

Olga told Milena she had seen her delirious, running wildly through hospital corridors, which only now confirmed for Milena that Olga had been hospitalized at the same time. Also, Olga had never revealed she had been slapped by the German SS officer when the two young women had been individually interrogated in Gorizia.

Vilmica recently gave Milena astonishing information about their transport to Germany in February 1945. That train was the very last transport to leave from their region—the last to make its way over a rail system which was being destroyed as it traveled across war-torn Germany to deposit its final prisoners. It was with sadness that they recalled the death on the transport of the elderly woman whose husband had been left at the Mauthausen concentration camp.

In turn, Milena told Vilmica of the woman who had, amazingly, been given permission to visit her sister on a farm near the train station she remembers as Dresden. Milena had hoped Vilmica could have confirmed that it had indeed been Dresden; however, since she had been in a different cattle car, she was unaware. It is ironic that while Milena had only seen a serene countryside dotted with fields, only about a week earlier the city of Dresden had been the target of the most destructive Allied bombing of the war.

The 70th anniversary of the end of World War II has helped to evoke these kinds of indelible memories for survivors whose information can continue to be recorded so that the world can never forget. Many, such as Vilmica, have worked for many years to keep the memory of the Holocaust and the injustice of the Fascist era alive.

Figure 29. Vilmica and Milena at the train station of Gorizia for the anniversary of one of the first battles of the Partisan Resistance against the Germans on September 12, 1943 (2014)

CHAPTER 2

The Concentration Camps

Understanding Milena's experience at Bergen-Belsen

Throughout the years after World War II, continued information has been released about the atrocities committed by the Nazis at Bergen-Belsen. This camp, which had been used to house POWs, was established within the Nazi system in 1943 as a "detention camp" for Jewish exchange prisoners. "Initially, the conditions under which prisoners were held at Bergen-Belsen were considerably better than at other concentration camps. The hostages had to be kept alive so they could be exchanged."[30] However, after the status of Bergen-Belsen changed within the camp system and it underwent conversions and expansions over its few years of existence, it represented the worst example of conditions among the Nazi concentration camps. After British Army units liberated the camp and released the "terrible pictures," "the name of Bergen-Belsen has since then stood as a symbol for the worst atrocities and inhumane barbarity of the Nazi system of concentration camps."[31]

The deteriorating conditions at Bergen-Belsen were due to several factors. From late 1944 to early 1945, evacuation transports from other concentration camps, impending the advance of Allied troops from the west and the Russian forces from the east, caused a tremendous increase in the number of inmates at Bergen-Belsen.[32] "From December 1944, at least 85,000 men, women and children were taken to Bergen-Belsen on more than 100 transports."[33]

Also, in early December 1944, Josef Kramer, previously commandant of the Auschwitz-Birkenau camp, took over the command of Bergen-Belsen. Along with his staff and the first-time presence of SS women guards there, Kramer transformed Bergen-Belsen into a "proper" concentration camp.[34] Milena's experience at the camp during this time of overcrowding exemplifies all accounts that Bergen-Belsen "lacked all facilities for receiving such numbers of prisoners ...."[35]

In spite of the many expansions that had occurred at Bergen-Belsen over the years, the shortage of space to accommodate these newly transported prisoners contributed to continuously worsening conditions.[36] "Prisoners who had come to know a whole range of German concentration camps and then got to Bergen-Belsen called it the dirtiest and most unhygienic of all German camps ...."[37] Huts had become so crowded that people were squeezed together, often competing for even a spot to lie down on the bare floor.[38] Prisoners received starvation rations, which, by then, were often depleted for days at a time due to these increased numbers.

During the days before the British liberation, the food supply stopped completely.[39] The camp administration had not allowed the repair of unusable water taps, and in some cases drinking water was only available from dirty cisterns.[40] "In the last days before the camp was handed over to the English, there was no water in the entire camp at all because a bomb had hit and rendered useless the power works whose electricity ran the pumping station."[41] These are the deplorable conditions Milena encountered at Bergen-Belsen during the last months before the end of the war.

Exhaustion, starvation from inadequate rations and the spread of disease resulted in extremely high mortality rates. March 1945, brought the highest number at 18,168, including those who died on incoming transports.[42] It was during these last months that Anne Frank, who has become an icon for the millions who suffered in the Holocaust, died of typhus at Bergen-Belsen, along with her sister Margot. The epidemic was responsible for many of the approximately 35,000 who perished between January and mid-April 1945.[43]

The conditions which Milena witnessed over the last few months of the camp's existence could only be described as an "inferno."[44] By March, bodies were stacked on piles in or near huts because "the number of victims exceeded the capacity of the camp's crematorium."[45] Due to the hundreds of additional deaths daily, "by the beginning of April, thousands of bodies were lying about in the camp area—green and swollen by the spring sun, in all stages of decomposition ....".[46] Within this scene of inhumanity, some prisoners fought to survive in the midst of horror. Others, overcome by sickness and exhaustion, simply lost their will to live and passed away without notice, their still bodies pulled from the huts upon discovery the next morning.

When the British arrived at Bergen-Belsen on April 15, they were completely unprepared for the horrific condition of the camp and its initially 60,000 survivors.[47] In some cases, 600 to 1000 people occupied a hut suitable for only 100. They found signs of filled-in mass graves, an open pit half-full of corpses and thousands of dead bodies lying throughout the camp.[48] The British took pictures and film to document a scene that defied description. These have been released gradually over time, and bear witness to the unspeakable war crimes committed at Bergen-Belsen.

"On April 17, thousands of emaciated and already decaying corpses began to be buried in huge mass graves. Captured SS personnel were made to do this macabre work."[49] At this time, Milena had been too weak to observe the scene her friends in the camp had been describing to her.

Evacuation of the camp did not begin until April 24. Because the British liberators had to deal with the typhus epidemic, which needed to be contained, Bergen-Belsen had not been evacuated like other camps. Instead, negotiations placed it in a neutral zone, as Allied and German military leaders feared spread of the typhus to both fighting troops and the civilian population. German *Wehrmacht* soldiers, as well as a unit of

Hungarian soldiers, had replaced the SS to keep the inmates within the camp.[50] Even though the camp had been officially liberated, shots were fired to maintain order and prevent starving prisoners from raiding food supplies.[51] As Milena described, liberation had not become a reality for the sick, starving prisoners remaining in those vile conditions. After the British arrived, food and medical relief followed within days, but in spite of their best efforts, 14,000 more prisoners died during the several weeks following liberation of the camp.[52] Approximately 2,000 of these former inmates perished as a result of inappropriate food intake for the starving.[53] Medical equipment was installed in the nearby barracks of the *Wehrmacht* military camp, which became an improvised hospital for sick prisoners. "On 21 May the whole camp had been evacuated, and in a solemn ceremony the last hut was set on fire with a flame-thrower and burnt to the ground."[54]

Shortly before the liberation of the camp, the SS destroyed all registers of inmates, leaving unanswered questions for many relatives on the fate of their loved ones. The staff at the Bergen-Belsen Memorial has been attempting to reconstruct data on the 120,000 estimated former prisoners of Bergen-Belsen. Their database currently includes more than 50,000 former prisoners.[55] Although Olga had been entered, Milena and her distant cousin, Vida, who Milena witnessed dying in *Revier*, have just recently been added to this number.

In quest of information on Milena's father at Neuengamme

In the search to learn more about Jožef Gulin, Milena's father and my grandfather, I visited Dachau concentration camp, where staff photocopied the transfer record of *Giuseppe Gulin* (Jožef's registered Italian name) to Neuengamme on October 22, 1944. I had been unfamiliar with this camp until the fall of 2012, when I traveled to the Neuengamme Concentration Camp Memorial in southeast Hamburg, Germany to see where my grandfather had ultimately died. This camp was nearly as large as Ravensbrück Concentration Camp for Women. Although it had over 100,000 prisoners among its main camp and the 76 satellite camps, and mortality rates higher than Buchenwald and Ravensbrück, Neuengamme remains less known than most other camps in the Nazi system.[56]

Formerly a satellite camp of Sachsenhausen, Neuengamme became an independent concentration camp in 1940. Its site at an old brick factory upon approximately 141 acres provided clay to "manufacture bricks for monumental buildings the Nazis wanted to construct in Hamburg."[57] Through what the SS referred to as "extermination through labor," work was carried out by exploited prisoners under severe conditions which often caused death from exhaustion.[58] The "regime of violence" included maltreatment, starvation rations, inadequate clothes for the cold, damp climate and work under constant surveillance with the threat of beatings from *Kapos* to increase output.[59] From these intolerable conditions to prisoner execution and murder from Nazi medical experimentation, the inmates of

Neuengamme were faced with the prospect of death on a daily basis.

At the main camp and its sub-camps throughout northern Germany, inmates provided slave labor in construction, armament production and other work details to aid the German wartime economy.[60] After Allied air raids, prisoners were also used to clear rubble and defuse bombs in Hamburg and other nearby cities.[61] Particularly difficult conditions were faced by those assigned to the Dove-Elbe detail, an ambitious project to make a five-kilometer stagnant arm of the Elbe River navigable by making it broader and deeper. Excavating a canal with a harbor basin allowed barges to transport bricks from the factory to Hamburg, as well as to supply coal and other materials to the camp. This work detail, considered the "death commando," was one of the worst and most dreaded.[62] Living conditions at Neuengamme deteriorated near the end of the war. Frequent new arrivals caused overcrowding, which contributed to the spread of disease. While the average mortality rate in 1943 was 332 deaths per month, during the month of December 1944, alone, 2675 deaths were recorded.[63]

When the British arrived on May 2 to liberate the prisoners of Neuengamme, they found it empty.[64] On March 24, 1945 the SS had begun to evacuate the entire Neuengamme camp system. Thousands were sent to Bergen-Belsen or other "reception camps" by train transport or death march. Danish and Norwegian prisoners were rescued by the Danish and Swedish Red Cross according to prior negotiation.[65] Twenty Jewish children, who had been taken from their parents at Auschwitz

203

and subjected to medical experimentation at Neuengamme, were murdered on April 20 at the evacuated satellite camp at the former school on Bullenhuser Damm.[66]   Nine thousand prisoners who were crammed on ships because there were no more reception camps available were accidentally bombed during a British air raid to stop German troops from escaping across the Baltic Sea.   Only 450 of these former prisoners survived.[67]   At the main camp, a work detail remained behind to clean up in order "to erase the traces of the crimes committed there."[68] The SS destroyed nearly all files and documents. On May 2, just before the British arrived, the last prisoners and SS had left the camp.[69] It has been assumed that the number of deaths at the Neuengamme camp system exceeds the 42,900 deaths for which there is evidence.[70]

According to Susanne Wald, employee at the Neuengamme Concentration Camp Memorial and authority on the subject, Italian prisoners (except for Soviets and Jews) found themselves lowest in the hierarchy at Neuengamme, which affected their ability to survive.[71] This was a result of Italy's war alliances, as well as the prisoners' late arrival into the camp.

Almost all the Italian prisoners at Neuengamme arrived at the camp after the Armistice of September 8, 1943.[72] Prior to that, Fascist Italy had been an Axis Power and ally of Nazi Germany. After Italy surrendered to the Allies, the German forces immediately moved troops into northern Italy. Italian soldiers, partisans and those civilians in the German occupied areas were at risk for arrest and deportation. More than 38,000 from Italy and its territory were deported to concentration and extermination camps throughout Germany during the twenty months of the German occupation. About 8,000 of these were Jews, and most of the remaining 30,000 were considered political prisoners, usually affiliated with the Resistance.[73] Most of these, such as Milena's father, were classified as "*Schutzhäftlinge,*" or those "detained for security reasons."[74]

All the later arriving deportees to Neuengamme had to cope with camp conditions, which by that time had become quite unbearable. In addition, they were placed in the worst and most difficult or dangerous work details because the assignments providing a greater possibility of survival had been taken.[75] According to Wald, most Italian arrivals were only briefly held at the main camp until they were assigned to a work detail at one of the satellite camps.[76] The mortality rate among the Italian inmates was particularly high.[77] I learned that *Giuseppe Gulin's* transport from Dachau, arriving at Neuengamme on October 22, 1944, had a total of 2000 deportees. According to an incomplete death list, 130 out of the approximately 370 Italians who had been on this transport died.[78]

As a consequence of Italy's surrender, the SS humiliated, degraded and vilified the Italian deportees as traitors from the moment they arrived. They were called *Banditen*, a term used to refer to partisans or others associated with the Resistance Movement. The Italians had to wear a red triangle with the letter 'I', and upon arrival, these male inmates were marked with the unmistakable sign of their status by shaving a large strip down to their skin from their nape to their forehead.[79]

According to former inmate, Miloš Poljanšek, a Slovene who arrived along with Italians on a September 1943 transport, *"Quando ci siamo messi in marcia dalla stazione ferroviaria per arrivare al lager, lungo la strada c'erano uomini, bambini, ma soprattuto donne, ci lanciavano insulti, non li abbiamo nemmeno capiti tutti, e ci hanno persino sputato addosso"*[80] [When we set off from the railroad station for the concentration camp, along the road there were men, children but mostly women, who shouted insults at us, all of which we didn't even comprehend, and they even spat at us].

Besides facing maltreatment by the SS, Italians deported to Neuengamme soon after the Armistice temporarily faced hostility and discrimination from fellow inmates who called them "fascist" and "Mussolini." At the beginning, these fellow inmates perceived them as citizens of Fascist Italy, Nazi Germany's ally, and Fascist Italy had played a role in repressing the Resistance in occupied areas of Europe.[81] Because the Italians at Neuengamme numbered only about 1200, and they were often scattered throughout the satellite camps, their experience in those early months after the Armistice was often isolating.[82]

One exception to this was a group of Italian women who had managed to remain together at the satellite camp of Salzgitter-Bad. Their solidarity had provided them with greater courage to face the hard life in the camp.[83]

A small number of the inmates, such as Milena's father, were not really Italians, but part of the Slovenian minority population who had suffered under fascism in Italy. With the hostile reaction immediately after the Armistice, these deportees must have especially found themselves suffering as persecuted among the persecuted. As a greater number of Italian partisans arrived on transports to Neuengamme, and were recognized as Resistance fighters, the inmates' antagonism toward Italian deportees ended.

There are still unanswered questions about Jožef Gulin's life since the sad day my aunt watched Tata's transport leave Gorizia. Although I don't know to which camp he was assigned in Neuengamme, after the war a former inmate from a neighboring town told the family that their father had been seen working in a swampy area, perhaps picking reeds for baskets. From this research and the information from the witness who saw him on a stretcher towards the end of the war, I surmise he must have died in the early spring of 1945, most likely at one of the satellite camps of Neuengamme. Since the family had received this anecdotal information about their father from former prisoners of Neuengamme, I can only hope he had experienced companionship during his last months of suffering.

Discovering Fascist Concentration Camps

Although the family had assumed that his transport traveled directly to Germany, Red Cross records show *Giuseppe Gulin* did not arrive in Dachau until September 25, 1944. Puzzled by where he had been detained during the three- to four-month interim, I embarked upon a search of Fascist Italy's little-known concentration camps, as well as the German camp of San Sabba.

207

Between the years 1942 and 1943, many Slovenian and Croatian civilians, suspected of supporting or giving aid to the partisans, were deported to Italian concentration camps. These deportees, whose homes were often looted and burned down, included men, women, children and the elderly. The Fascist regime was responsible for building over fifty locations of internment. Fascist camps with a large number of Slovenian prisoners included Arbe on the island of Rab, Gonars, Padova, Treviso and Renicci. According to data found in the *Archivio Centrale di Stato* (Central Archives of the State) in Rome, by the end of October 1942, the number of Slovenian civilian deportees just among these five camps had already reached about 20,000. Nevertheless, because there were so many other locations of internment, this number would be much greater. Especially at Arbe, the death rate due to hunger, exposure and disease was, for long periods, greater than in the worst Nazi concentration camps, excluding those of extermination.[84]

Ending the search at Risiera of San Sabba

By October 1943, when the Adriatic Littoral area came under the direct administration of Hitler's Third Reich, a rice-refining factory complex located in suburban Trieste became a notorious Nazi German concentration camp. This facility, the Risiera of San Sabba, temporarily used for the detention of Jews and Italian soldiers captured after September 8, was transformed into the only fully-fledged Nazi extermination camp in Italy.[85]

At that time, SS General Odilo Globočnik, who had been responsible for the death camps of Treblinka, Belzec and

Sobibor in Poland, was transferred to the region of Trieste, and evidence suggests his extermination techniques were applied at San Sabba.[86] With extermination practiced, above all, on partisans and political prisoners, killing was typically carried out by German SS through beating, gassing, shooting and strangling.[87] Because this camp was located in the suburbs, the roar of engines, loud military marching music, along with dogs made to bark, concealed any noise from victims who were gassed by the carbon monoxide produced by the engine of a truck introduced into a sealed room.[88] The victims at the Risiera are estimated to be 5,000 killed and 20,000 deported and imprisoned.[89]

I have recently discovered Milena's father was among those imprisoned at San Sabba. Red Cross records show he was transported to Dachau from Trieste. We were informed that there were two possibilities of detainment in Trieste—the jail or San Sabba. After searching in vain through the archives of prisoners at the Trieste jail, a reliable source at the San Sabba Civic Museum told us that the absence of the name *Giuseppe Gulin* in those jail records indicates he most certainly spent his first months of internment at San Sabba. Even after more than seventy years, it makes my mother sad to learn that her father was so close to home, and the family was unaware.

On the night of April 29, 1945, as Yugoslav troops approached Trieste, the Nazis dynamited the crematorium oven at the Risiera before they fled.[90] Due to the situation in Trieste after the war and the occupation by the Allied Military Government, official action for those responsible for war crimes at San Sabba was blocked by the occupation forces. More than thirty years passed before any trials took place.[91]

CHAPTER 3

The Regional Jewish Population

Although this book has focused on the Slovenian minority in Italy, the persecution of Jews living in this part of Italy must be addressed. The Jewish population in Gorizia had never been more than 300 residents, but their role had been notable in social, business and intellectual circles of the community.[92] By contrast, in the late 1930s Trieste's Jewish community had numbered about 5,000. When Fascist Italy introduced racial legislation against this population in 1938, many Jews from Trieste decided to leave the country. Nevertheless, from those remaining in the city, the Nazis succeeded in deporting more than 700 to extermination camps, out of which no more than twenty returned.[93]

In spite of their own suffering, examples of Jewish empathy toward the discrimination of the Slovenian minority can be found in books written by regional authors. Aldo Pavia and Antonella Tiburzi wrote the memoir of Ida Marcheria, a fourteen year-old Jewish girl from Trieste who was deported to Auschwitz. In her book, *Non perdonerò mai* (*I Will Never Forgive*), Marcheria described the deplorable manner in which the fascists treated the Slovenes. She felt that the many people from Trieste who spoke Slovene had the right to speak their language, even though the fascists did not see it that way. Marcheria recalled that the Slovenes had been victims for years, but after September 8, they faced more frequent attacks and deportations, and many were finally killed.[94]

In another book, *Valdirose: memorie della comunità ebraica di Gorizia.* (*Valdirose: Memory of the Jewish Community of Gorizia*), Gorizia resident Marcello Morpurgo believed it impossible that, under the Fascist regime, his rights as an Italian citizen would be restricted because of his Jewishness. He belonged to the Organization for Young Fascists, and was in his final year of university in September 1938 when Mussolini came to Gorizia for his official visit. Morpurgo attended with little enthusiasm, but carried out his assignment when put in charge of a group of Slovenian boys in the school yard. When the boys spoke Slovenian among themselves, Morpurgo was disturbed that the authorities scolded the boys for speaking their home language. He reveled in noncompliance by permitting them to continue, even though he had been instructed to prohibit this communication. Morpurgo felt that imposing such laws would only discourage loyalty of its citizens to the State.[95]

Figure 30 Postcard of Mussolini's September 20, 1938 visit to Gorizia with photomontage to exalt the presence of the crowd during his speech in Piazza Vittoria. XVI indicates Mussolini's 16 years of rule. (Translation: "Fascist and warlike Gorizia acclaims the Founder of the Empire.")
Courtesy of *Isonzo-Soča, Giornale di Frontiera*

The following day, Mussolini addressed the people of Trieste. He told the crowd that Jews who had been loyal Italian citizens would have no reason for concern.[96] Yet only a few days later, the racial laws were enacted against them. The Jews were shocked, for they had played an important role in the community, especially in the city of Trieste, since the days of the Austro-Hungarian Empire. Many were influential citizens who had worked in professional occupations and had held public office. With the promulgation, Jews were prohibited from owning houses or companies. They could no longer enter the medical, law or educational professions, nor could they attend schools or enter universities.[97]

Because Morpurgo had already been attending the university, he was allowed to complete his education, but with little hope of securing employment.[98] Although it was prohibited for non-Jews to hire Jewish employees, he got a job at a ceramic tile company in Gorizia owned by a Slovene—the same company at which Nino and Pepe had worked for a short time.[99]

"After Italy joined World War II in June 1940, Italian anti-Jewish policy worsened. New decrees against the Jews were added to the racial laws of 1938, and an anti-Semitic propaganda campaign began."[100] Under Mussolini's regime, the Italians had not deported the Jews to concentration camps from Italy or from the occupied territory of Yugoslavia. Instead, in 1942, Jews in Gorizia had been taken for forced labor—men in the lumber yards and women to sew.[101] This changed after Mussolini's regime collapsed in September 1943, and the Germans occupied Italy. During this time, "[a]pproximately one-fifth of the 44,000 Jews living in Italy were sent to the concentration and death camps."[102]

In Gorizia, the 155 members of the synagogue had been reduced to about 80 by 1943.[103] Just as the deportations for the Slavic population had increased after the Italian Armistice on September 8, it was on the night of November 23, 1943, that the 49 mostly women, children and elderly Jews found remaining in Gorizia were arrested and deported to Auschwitz. "Very few returned ...."[104] On a marble memorial tablet in the courtyard at the entrance of the synagogue are inscribed the names of the 45 who died, including an infant of 3 months and 19 days. Among those not arrested were some young Jews who had joined the Partisan Resistance and others who had gone into hiding or had fled. Morpurgo was one who, in 1943 after the Armistice,

214

aligned himself with Tito's partisans. "We show our solidarity to whomever fights against fascism," he proclaimed.[105]

At the end of the war, the synagogue was reopened by the American Blue Devil 88th Infantry Division for worship by its approximately 400 Jewish soldiers. By 1959, due to the small number of Jewish residents in Gorizia, the Israelite Community of Gorizia became part of the Israelite Community of Trieste.[106] Due to the changing border after World War II, Gorizia's historic Jewish cemetery, containing approximately 900 tombstones, now stands on the Slovenian side of the border in the Nova Gorica suburb of Rožna Dolina (Valdirose in Italian), for which Morpurgo names his book, *Valdirose*. Today the synagogue in Gorizia, standing on Via G.I. Ascoli in the former Jewish section of the city, has no Jewish membership, but remains as a monument to those who perished. The garden of the synagogue is dedicated to the infant, Bruno Farber, the youngest deportee who died in Auschwitz.

Figure 31. The Synagogue of Gorizia on Via Ascoli built in 1756 (1940)
Courtesy of Claudio Bulfoni, Synagogue of Gorizia

Figure 32. The garden of the synagogue, dedicated to Bruno Farber, with its 18th century wrought-iron gate, thought to have been the old gate to the Jewish ghetto in Gorizia.

Figure 33. Plaque in garden dedicated to Bruno Farber. Translation: "This garden is dedicated to Bruno Farber, son of Jews from Gorizia—deported and killed at Auschwitz at the age of 3 months. November 7, 1943 - February 26, 1944."

Chapter 4

Living "On the Edge of a Country"

Being a Slovene within Italy can be complex. For many ethnic Slovenes in this region, the process of constructing their identities has been a lifelong journey. Although some Slovenes have resisted assimilation in a desire to maintain their language and culture, others, influenced to believe Italian is the superior culture, have disregarded their Slovenian roots. For many of the older generation, life has become easier simply by trying to forget the past.

If Italy had taken greater responsibility for its war crimes and atrocities committed against the Slovenes and other Slavic minorities during the Fascist era, perhaps this group could more easily come to terms with its history. As long as there are people on the political Right who deny history and continue prejudicial rhetoric against Slovenes, resolution is difficult. Boris Pahor, author and centenarian, is an ethnic Slovene who continues to raise awareness about the atrocities committed under Fascist Italy. His books about the era and his experiences in Nazi concentration camps have given voice to all Slovenes who demand Italy take responsibility for these war crimes.

Ethnic Slovenes in this region are Italian by citizenship, but some still feel their place in Italian society remains peripheral. They do not completely belong to either the Slovenian or Italian cultures, but are a distinct blend of both. Physically, as well as psychologically, they have lived "on the edge of a country" in this location so close to the border that Italians in other parts of the nation may forget Gorizia is really part of Italy.

Dr. Paolo Fonda, an ethnic-Slovene and resident of Trieste, is a psychoanalyst who has studied the social dynamics within the region. According to Dr. Fonda, unlike Italians in other parts of Italy such as Milan or Rome, who take their Italianness for granted, such is often not the case for an Italian from Gorizia or Trieste.[107] Living on a border creates individuals whose origins are less distinct. Moreover, and often unwittingly, they have absorbed elements of the neighboring culture. Fonda explains that ever since Gorizia became part of Italy, there has been a tendency to conceal anything that is not Italian, whether it be Austrian or Slovenian. In order to strengthen one's Italian identity in this border community, there is often a subconscious need to deny or resist any foreign element. For some residents of this city, the Slovenian presence may, therefore, be perceived as a threat to their image of what it means to be Italian.[108]

Many ethnic-Slovenes, Dr. Fonda explains, have in recent years, made progress towards developing a more complete identity. In some ways, the challenges of a difficult history have enabled them to construct and strengthen self-image. This awareness has more easily allowed them to be a part of the greater Italian community without feeling a betrayal of self. Today they are more often living their bilingual and bicultural identity instead of suppressing it.[109]

In the region today, there is a population of 50,000 to 100,000 Slovenes, who can be characterized with various levels of belonging to this ethnic group. Their relationship with the Italian community varies according to whether they live in Trieste, Gorizia or in smaller towns and rural areas.

Dario Stasi, regional journalist, author and advocate for tolerance and multicultural unity, has attempted to bridge the divide that remains between these two cultures. His bilingual journal, *Isonzo-Soča, Giornale di Frontiera / Časopis Na Meji*, the first of its kind in Gorizia, has educated and raised awareness about this region for over twenty-five years. Written in both languages, Italian and Slovene, the title of the journal comes from the name of the emerald-colored river, *Isonzo* in Italian and *Soča* in Slovene which crosses both countries. The journal often focuses on controversial topics to encourage community discourse about issues on which the two groups have not yet come to terms.

Another attempt to find commonality and understanding between the Slovenes' and Italians' past occurred when the history of this region was reviewed by *Commissione Mista Storico-Culturale Italo-Slovena*, a commission formed in 1993, to write a shared interpretation of historical facts. Twenty historians—ten Italians and ten Slovenes—collaborated to analyze the events that took place in this area from the late 1800s to the 1950s. In 2001, they produced a thirty-page document—an instrument with which to interpret the recent history of two peoples. Although officially accepted and printed by the Slovenian government, it was dismissed by Italian officials who argued that "in a democracy there could not be a single, official history" and, furthermore, it was not the function of government to provide it.[110] The document was only printed locally by the daily paper of Trieste and Gorizia, *Il Piccolo*, and by some local historical journals. Subsequently, it was distributed by the journal *Isonzo-Soča*.

Of course, the passing of years has brought significant change. The memories of war and of the tensions which existed between the Slovenian minority and Italians have faded. After Slovenia led the fight for independence from Yugoslavia in 1991, it established a democratic republic. With communism gone, there has been less hatred toward Slovenia. This, too, has allowed the Slovenian minority in Italy to live their Slovenian ethnicity with greater comfort. Three years after Slovenia was accepted into the European Union in 2004, the border between these two countries disappeared, and relations have improved. For example, some Italians, especially of mixed Italian and Slovenian marriages, send their children to Slovenian schools in Gorizia to learn the language of their neighboring country. Also, Italians' attitude towards Slovenia has changed, and increasingly more people visit the country to shop, eat in restaurants and take advantage of all Nova Gorica has to offer.

Thanks to those who work to increase awareness of the past and instill hope for the future, a city such as Gorizia can come to terms with its history and move forward. Over time, there may even come the acknowledgment that *Gorizia,* derived from the Slovenian word *gorica*, meaning "little mountain," is also a city with Slovenian roots. It is the hope of tolerant Slovenes and Italians that their city serve as a role model of coexistence and cooperation within Europe and that its residents uphold and cherish Gorizia as a rich multicultural city.

Figure 34. The medieval-century castle sits above Gorizia on the hill ("little mountain") from which the city gets its name.

NOTES

1. Friuli-Venezia Giulia, as it is currently known, is comprised of Venezia Giulia and Friuli. Friuli, with its city of Udine, had been under Habsburg rule until 1866 when it became part of the Kingdom of Italy. This memoir takes place in the region of Venezia Giulia, the territory that remained under Habsburg rule until the end of World War I.

2. The Isonzo-Soča River flows from the Julian Alps to the Adriatic Sea passing through western Slovenia and northeastern Italy.

3. Otto Luthar, ed., *The Land Between, A History of Slovenia*, trans. Manca Gašperšič (Frankfurt: Peter Lang, 2008), 380.

4. Glenda Sluga, *The Problem of Trieste and the Italo-Yugoslav Border* (Albany: State University of New York, 2001), 42.

5. Luthar, ed., *The Land Between*, 398.

6. Ibid.

7. Boris Pahor, *Necropolis*, trans. Michael Biggins (Champaign: Dalkey Archive Press, 2010), 17.

8. Borut Klabjan, "Slavic Terrorists, Fascist Propaganda and the Perception of the Slovene and Croatian Minorities in Italy" (8th Annual Kokkalis Graduate Student Workshop,

Harvard University, Cambridge, Massachusetts, February 3, 2006), 4.

9. Luthar, ed., *The Land Between*, 399.

10. "Uno Sguardo alla Storia," in *Isonzo-Soča, Giornale di Frontiera*, no.82-83 (2009): 6-25.

11. Luciano Patat, *Terra di frontiera, Fascismo, guerra e dopoguerra nell' Isontino e nella Bassa friulana* (Gorizia: Centro Isontino di Ricerca e Documentazione Storica e Sociale "Leopoldo Gasparini," 2002), 40.

12. Elio Apih, *Risiera di San Sabba* (Comune di Trieste Civici Musei di Storia ed Arte, 2000), 39.

13. Luthar, ed., *The Land Between*, 399.

14. Ibid.

15. The Allied forces within Europe included France, Great Britain, Russia, Greece, Luxembourg, The Netherlands, Norway, Poland, Turkey and Yugoslavia. The United States joined the Allies on December 7, 1941 after the attack on Pearl Harbor by Japan.

16. Luthar, ed., *The Land Between*, 417-418.

17. Apih, *Risiera di San Sabba*, 37.

18. Ibid., 39.

19. Marcello Morpurgo, *Valdirose: memorie della comunità ebraica di Gorizia* (Udine: Del Bianco,1986), 130.

20. Frederick M. Shaine, trans., wrote "Introduction by the Translator," in *And No Quarter: An Italian Partisan in World War II: Memoirs of Giovanni Pesce* (Ohio University Press, 1972), 3.

21. Boris M. Gombać, and Dario Mattiussi, *La deportazione dei civili sloveni e croati nei campi di concentramento italiani 1942-1943, I campi dei confine orientale* (Gorizia: "L.Gasparini," Centro Isontino di Ricerca e Documentazione Storica e Sociale, 2004), 35.

22. The people classified as "Gypsies" were Sinti and Roma people who were persecuted by the Nazis. Racist policies against these groups were similar to those against the Jews. Milena encountered many Sinti and Roma women at Bergen-Belsen, and lived side by side with many in the huts. A large number of them arrived on evacuation transports from other camps during the last months of the war.

23. Bogdan C. Novak, *Trieste 1941-1954, The Ethnic, Political, and Ideological Struggle* (Chicago: University of Chicago Press, 1970), 179-180.

24. Bernard Meares, "Where the Balkans Begin: The Slovenes in Trieste" (1998): 22. http://miran.pecenik.com/ts/balkan/balkan0.htm. Accessed July 18, 2009.

25. John P. Delaney, *The Blue Devils in Italy: a History of the 88th Infantry Division in World War II*, (Washington D.C.: Washington Infantry Journal Press, 1947), 253.

26. "Oltre il confine/Čez mejo," in *Isonzo Soca, Giornale di Frontiera*, no. 57 (April-May, 2004): 11.

27. Francesco Palermo and Giulia Predonzani, "The Slovene Minority in Italy: Unfinished Protection," *Osservatorio Balcani e Caucas* (October 28, 2008). http://www.balcanicaucaso.org.

28. Anja Medved and Nadja Velušček, *Mesto na travniku: videoesej o Novi Gorici*, directed by Radovan Čok (Nova Gorica: Moja Meja, 2002), DVD.

29. Ibid.

30. Habbo Knoch, ed., *Bergen-Belsen Historical Site and Memorial*, trans. Georg Felix Harsch and Jessica Spengler (Celle: Lower Saxony Memorials Foundation, 2011), 21.

31. Eberhard Kolb, *Bergen-Belsen From 1943 to 1945*, trans. Gregory Claeys and Christine Lattek (Göttingen, Germany: Vandenhoeck & Ruprecht, 1985), 11.

32. Knoch, ed., *Bergen-Belsen Historical Site and Memorial*, 25-26.

33. Ibid., 26.

34. Kolb, *Bergen-Belsen*, 37-38.

35. Ibid., 38.

36. Ibid., 39-40.

37. Ibid., 42.

38. Ibid., 43.

39. Knoch, ed., *Bergen-Belsen Historical Site and Memorial*, 27.

40. Kolb, *Bergen-Belsen*, 42-43.

41. Ibid., 43.

42. Ibid., 39.

43. Ibid.

44. Ibid., 38.

45. Knoch, *Bergen-Belsen Historical Site and Memorial*, 26.

46. Kolb, *Bergen-Belsen*, 46.

47. Ibid., 47-49.

48. Ibid., 48.

49. Ibid.

50. Ibid., 47.

51. Ben Shephard, *After Daybreak: The Liberation of Bergen-Belsen* (New York: Schocken Books, 2005), 35-36.

52. Habbo Knoch, preface to *Bergen-Belsen: Wehrmacht POW Camp 1940-1945, Concentration Camp 1943-1945, Displaced Persons Camp 1945-1950, Catalogue accompanying the permanent exhibition*, edited by Lower Saxony Memorials Foundation, trans. George Felix Harsch (Göttingen: Wallstein Verlag, 2010), 9.

53. Shephard, *After Daybreak*, 40.

54. Kolb, *Bergen-Belsen*, 49.

55. Knoch, *Bergen-Belsen Historical Site and Memorial*, 74-75.

56. Detlef Garbe, "Il Campo di Neuengamme nel Sistema Concentrazionario Nazista," in *Il Libro dei Deportati, Volume III*, eds., Mantelli, Brunello and Nicola Tranfaglia (Milano: Mursia, 2010), 387.

57. Karin Schawe, ed., *KZ-Gedenkstätte Neuengamme*, trans. Georg Felix Harsch (Hamburg: Neuengamme Concentration Camp Memorial, 2010), 10.

58. Garbe, "Il Campo de Neuengamme," 387.

59. Ibid., 390-391.

60. Schawe, *KZ-Gedenkstätte-Neuengamme*, 10.

61. Ibid., 34.

62. Detlef Garbe and Wolfgang Stiller, eds., *Zeitspuren KZ-Gedenkstätte Neuengamme Die Ausstellungen*, trans. Georg Felix Harsch, Michael Hale and Jessica Spengler (Bremen: Temmen, 2005), 68.

63. Garbe, "Il Campo Neuengamme," 403.

64. Schawe, ed., *KZ-Gedenkstätte-Neuengamme*, 19.

65. Ibid., 42.

66. Iris Groschek and Kristina Vagt, *Gedenkstätte Bullenhuser Damm*, trans. Georg Felix Harsch (Hamburg: Neuengamme Concentration Camp Memorial, 2011), 13-17.

67. Schawe, ed., *KZ-Gedenkstätte-Neuengamme*, 44.

68. Groschek and Vagt, *Gedenkstätte Bullenhuser Damm*, 17.

69. Ibid.

70. Schawe, ed., *KZ-Gedenkstätte-Neuengamme*, 45.

71. Susanne Wald, "'E Tornai Vivo Dall'Inferno dei Morti,' Deportati italiani nel campo di concentramento di Neuengamme," in *Il Libro dei Deportati, Volume III*, eds. Brunello Mantelli and Nicola Tranfaglia (Mursia: 2010), 424.

72. Ibid., 425.

73. Alessandra Chiappano, *Essere donne nei Lager* (Istituto storico della resistenza e dell'età contemporanea in Ravenna e provincial: La Giuntina, 2009), 71.

74. Wald, "E Tornai Vivo Dall'Inferno dei Morti," 426.

75. Garbe, "Il Campo Neuengamme," 394.

76. Wald, "E Tornai Vivo Dall'Inferno dei Morti," 432.

77. Ibid., 424.

78. Ibid., 426-427.

79. Ibid., 422.

80. Ibid., 429.

81. Ibid., 423.

82. Ibid., 424.

83. Ibid.

84. Boris M. Gombać and Dario Mattiussi, *La deportazione dei civili sloveni e croati nei campi di concentramento italiani:1942-1943, I campi dei confine orientale*, (Gorizia: "L. Gasparini" Centro Isontino di Ricerca e Documentazione Storica e Sociale, 2004), 13.

85. Elio Apih, *Risiera di San* Sabba (Comune di Trieste: Civici Musei de Storia Ed Arte, 2000), 36.

86. Ibid., 37.

87. Ibid., 36.

88. *Risiera di San Sabba: Monumento Nazionale* (Comune di Trieste, 1995), 10.

89. Ibid., 40.

90. Apih, 40.

91. Ibid.

92. Claudio Bulfoni, "La Sinagoga di Gorizia" (Gorizia: Il Comune, 1987).

93. *Risiera di San Sabba: Monumento Nazionale*, 11.

94. Aldo Pavia and Antonella Tiburzi, *Non perdonerò mai* (Portogruaro, Venezia: nuova dimensione, 2006), 25.

95. Marcello Morpurgo, *Valdirose: memorie della communita ebraica di Gorizia* (Udine: Del Bianco,1986), 91-92.

96. Morpurgo, 202.

97. Ibid., 94-95.

98. Ibid., 97.

99. Ibid., 99.

100. Yad Vashem Photo Archives. 4613/82. http://www. yadvashem.org/yv/en/exhibitions/this_month/september/09.asp. Accessed August 5, 2009.

101. Claudio Bulfoni, Personal interview by author, Gorizia, October 13, 2011.

102. Yad Vashem Photo Archives.

103. Bulfoni, Personal interview.

104. Antonio Devetag, *Itinerario ebraico sulle tracce di Michelstaedter* (Cormons, Gorizia: Poligrafiche San Marco, Ottobre 2010), 41.

105. Morpurgo, *Valdirose,* 122.

106. Bulfoni, "La Sinagoga di Gorizia."

107. "Gorizia e Trieste in Psicoanalisi," in *Isonzo Soča, Giornale di Frontiera,* no. 6 (Inverno 1991): 2-4.

108. Ibid., 4-5.

109. Ibid., 7-8.

110. Stefano Lusa, "'Memory Day" Across the Border," *Osservatorio Balcani e Caucaso* (February 9, 2009). http:// www.balcanicaucaso.org.

HISTORICAL CHRONOLOGY

1500 - Gorizia (Gorica in Slovene), seat of the independent County of Gorizia since the 11th century, passes under the Austrian rule of the Habsburgs.

1867 - Austria-Hungary, or the Austro-Hungarian Empire, is established from the union of the Austrian Empire with the Kingdom of Hungary. Emperor Franz Josef continues the Habsburg rule of Gorizia, or Görz in German.

1914 - Austria-Hungary reaches its greatest size.

July 28, 1914 - Austria-Hungary declares war on Serbia and World War I begins.

April 26, 1915 - Italy signs the Treaty of London with Great Britain, France and Russia, and is secretly promised territory for joining the Allies.

May 23, 1915 - Italy declares war on Austria-Hungary and enters WWI on the side of the Allies.

August 8, 1916 - The Italian army conquers Gorizia in the 6th Battle of the Isonzo, but is later retaken by the Austrians. From June 1915 to November 1917, the Twelve Battles of the Isonzo are fought in the area surrounding Gorizia.

November 1916 - Franz Josef, Emperor of Austria, King of Hungary and the last significant Habsburg monarch dies.

October 31, 1918 - Austria-Hungary dissolves.

November 4, 1918 - World War I ends on the Italian Front after Austria-Hungary and Italy sign the Armistice of Villa Giusti. The Kingdom of Italy annexes the Adriatic Littoral according to terms of the London Pact.

November 11, 1918 - World War I ends on the Western Front after the Allies sign a ceasefire agreement with Germany at the eleventh hour, on the eleventh day, of the eleventh month. For most World War I Allied countries, this day is a national holiday known as Armistice Day or Remembrance Day. In the United States, after WWII and the Korean War, Armistice Day becomes Veterans Day to remember American veterans from all wars.

December 1, 1918 - The unified Yugoslav state called the Kingdom of Serbs, Croats and Slovenes is formed.

March 23, 1919 – Benito Mussolini, formerly editor of a Socialist Party newspaper, establishes the political movement of Fascism in Italy, whose action squads use organized violence against Slavic organizations and left-wing opponents.

September 10, 1919 - The Treaty of St. Germain is signed to formally dissolve the Austro-Hungarian Empire. This treaty officially gives the Austrian Littoral (Adriatic Littoral) to Italy.

July 13, 1920 - Fascist Blackshirts burn *Narodni Dom*, the Slovenian Cultural Center in Trieste. Fascism becomes a strong political force in Trieste.

November 12, 1920 - The Treaty of Rapallo is signed to settle disputes over the Adriatic Littoral territory from the dissolution of the Austrian Empire.

1922 - Italy claims Fiume (Rijeka in Slovene).

October 1922 - Benito Mussolini comes to power as the leader of the Fascist Party of Italy.

January 27, 1924 - The Treaty of Rome gives the city of Fiume to Italy. Under the Treaty of Rapallo it had been recognized as a free state. Rijeka is currently in Croatia.

1926 - All political parties other than the Fascist Party are prohibited in Italy.

1926 - Fascists assault *Trgovski Dom*, the Slovenian Cultural Center in Gorizia.

1929 - King Alexander I assumes power of the Kingdom of Serbs, Croats and Slovenes and renames the country Kingdom of Yugoslavia.

September 20, 1938 - Mussolini makes an official visit to Gorizia.

September, 1938 - The Jewish racial laws begin to be enacted in Italy.

September 1, 1939 - World War II begins when Germany attacks Poland.

June 10, 1940 - Italy enters WWII with the Axis Powers, alongside Nazi Germany.

April 6, 1941 - The Axis Powers attack Yugoslavia.

April 17, 1941 – The Yugoslav Army surrenders and the occupation of Yugoslavia begins.

April 1941 - Josip Broz Tito organizes the Partisan Resistance Army.

July 31, 1942 - Mussolini makes another visit to Gorizia.

July 1943 - The Allies invade Sicily.

July 25, 1943 - Mussolini is asked to resign by the King, and he is arrested and imprisoned on the Gran Sasso Mountain.

September 3, 1943 - Italy surrenders.

September 8, 1943 - The Italian Armistice is officially declared. The Italian military system collapses. Thousands of Italian soldiers are deported to Germany.

September 12, 1943 - Mussolini is freed from prison in an SS raid and meets with Hitler in Germany. A separate Republican government with headquarters at Salò on Lake Garda is set up.

September 12, 1943 - The Partisan Resistance fights their battle with German forces at the train station in Gorizia.

September 1943 - Germany occupies central and northern Italy with Fascist collaborators.

October 1, 1943 – The Adriatic Littoral officially becomes the German province of *Adriatisches Küstenland* under the direct administration of the Third Reich. This new German territory includes the provinces of Gorizia, Udine, Trieste, Pola, Fiume and Ljubljana.

October 13, 1943 - Italy declares war on Nazi Germany, its former Axis partner.

November 23, 1943 - All remaining Jews in Gorizia are arrested to be deported to Auschwitz.

January 27, 1945 - The Soviets liberate the remaining prisoners in Auschwitz who had not left on evacuation marches or transports to other Nazi concentration camps.

April 15, 1945 - British troops arrive at Bergen-Belsen and liberation begins.

April 24, 1945 - The Soviet Army surrounds Berlin.

April 28, 1945 - Captured Mussolini is shot by the partisans.

April 30, 1945 - Adolf Hitler commits suicide as the Soviet forces close in on his underground complex in Berlin.

May 1, 1945 - Tito's Yugoslav Partisan Resistance forces liberate Trieste (Trst in Slovene) and Gorizia.

May 2, 1945 - Soviets take the city of Berlin.

May 2, 1945 - British troops arrive to liberate the prisoners of Neuengamme, but find the concentration camp empty.

May 3, 1945 - WWII is over on all European fronts.

May 7, 1945 - Germany signs an unconditional surrender at Allied headquarters, Reims, France which takes effect May 8.

June, 1945 - The Allied Military Government occupies Venezia Giulia.

1945 - Yugoslavia becomes a Republic under communist rule with Josip Broz Tito as its leader.

November 1, 1945 - The American Blue Devil 88th Army Division occupies the region.

November 25, 1945 - The funeral of 112 partisans is held in Piazza Vittoria, Gorizia.

February 10, 1947 - The Treaty of Paris is signed, which delineates the boundary between the Republic of Italy and the Yugoslav Federal People's Republic.

September 15, 1947 - The Paris Peace Treaty provisions are put into effect.

1948 - The building of Nova Gorica begins.

1948 - Marshal Tito breaks ties with the Soviet Union and begins to develop the country's alternative model of socialism.

1952 - Nova Gorica is established as an urban municipality.

1954 - Trieste is turned over to Italy.

1980 - Marshal Josip Broz Tito dies.

June 1991 - Slovenia declares independence from Yugoslavia.

2001 - Protection of the Slovenian Minority Rights Act is passed by the Italian Parliament.

2004 - Slovenia is admitted to the European Union.

BIBLIOGRAPHY

Angelillo, Alfonso, Antonio Angelillo and Chiara Menato. "Il Confine Gorizia-Nova Gorica." *Isonzo-Soča, Giornale di Frontiera*, no. 10 (1993): 32-33.

Apih, Elio. *Risiera di San Sabba.* Comune di Trieste: Civici Musei de Storia Ed Arte, 2000.

Bulfoni, Claudio. *La Sinagoga di Gorizia.* Gorizia: Il Comune, 1987.

Chiappano, Alessandra; Istituto storico della resistenza e dell'età contemporanea in Ravenna e provincial. *Essere donne nei Lager.* Firenze: La Giuntina, 2009.

Cooke, Philip, ed. *The Italian Resistance, An anthology.* Manchester: Manchester University Press, 1997.

Delaney, John P. *The Blue Devils in Italy: a History of the 88th Infantry Division in World War II.* Washington D.C.:Washington Infantry Journal Press, 1947.

Delzell, Charles F. "The Italian Anti-Fascist Resistance in Retrospect: Three Decades of Historiography." *The Journal of Modern History,* 47, no. 1 (1975): 66-96.

Devetag, Antonio. *Itinerario ebraico sulle tracce di Michelstaedter.* Cormons (Gorizia): Poligrafiche San Marco, Ottobre 2010.

"Drnovsek Addresses Letter to Napolitano over Latest Foibe Spat." February 14, 2007. Republic of Slovenia Government Communication Office. http://www.ukom. gov.si/eng/slovenia/publications/slovenia-news/4343/4356/

Garbe, Detlef. "Il Campo de Neuengamme nel Sistema Concentrazionario Nazista." In *Il Libro dei Deportati, Volume III, La galassia concentrazionaria SS 1933-1945*, edited by Brunello Mantelli and Nicola Tranfaglia, 387-421. Milano: Mursia, 2010.

Garbe, Detlef and Wolfgang Stiller, eds. *Zeitspuren KZ-Gedenkstatte Neuengamme Die Ausstellungen*. Translated by Georg Felix Harsch, Michael Hale and Jessica Spengler. Bremen: Temmen, 2005.

Gombać, Boris M. and Dario Mattiussi. *La deportazione dei civili sloveni e croati nei campi di concentramento italiani 1942-1943, I campi dei confine orientale*. Gorizia: "L. Gasparini," Centro Isontino di Ricerca e Documentazione Storica e Sociale, 2004.

"Gorizia e Trieste in Psicoanalisi." In *Izonzo Soča, Giornale di Frontiera*, no. 6 (1991): 4-8.

Groschek, Iris and Kristina Vagt. *Gedenkstätte Bullenhuser Damm*. Edited by Karin Schawe. Translated by Georg Felix Harsch. Hamburg: Neuengamme Concentration Camp Memorial, 2011.

"Italian MEP Compares Foibe to Nazi Concentration Camp." April 19, 2005. Republic of Slovenia Government Communication Office. http://www.ukom.gov.si/eng/slovenia/publications/slovenia-news/1926/1946/.

Klabjan, Borut. "Slavic Terrorists, Fascist Propaganda and the Perception of the Slovene and Croatian Minorities in Italy." Presented at 8th Annual Kokkalis Graduate Student Workshop, Harvard University, Cambridge, Massachusetts, February 3, 2006.

Knoch, Habbo, ed. *Bergen-Belsen Historical Site and Memorial*. Translated by Georg Felix Harsch and Jessica Spengler. Celle: Lower Saxony Memorials Foundation, 2011.

Knoch, Habbo. Preface to *Bergen-Belsen: Wehrmacht POW Camp 1940-1945, Concentration Camp 1943-1945, Displaced Persons Camp 1945-1950, Catalogue accompanying the permanent exhibition*, edited by Lower Saxony Memorials Foundation. Translated by George Felix Harsch. Göttingen: Wallstein Verlag, 2010.

Kolb, Eberhard. *Bergen-Belsen From 1943 to 1945*. Translated by Gregory Claeys and Christine Lattek. Göttingen, Germany: Vandenhoeck & Ruprecht, 1985.

Komel, Igor, Jurij Paljk, Milan Pahor, Vili Prinčič, eds. *Trgovski Dom di Gorizia: cent'anni di presenza*. Slovenska Konzulta pri občini, 2007.

Luthar, Otto, ed. *The Land Between, A History of Slovenia*. Translated by Manca Gašperšič. Frankfurt: Peter Lang, 2008.

Lusa, Stefano. "'Memory Day' Across the Border." February 9, 2009. *Osservatorio Balcani e Caucaso*. http//www.balcanicaucaso.org.

Meares, Bernard. "Where the Balkans Begin: The Slovenes in Trieste." 1998. http://miran.pecenik.com/ts/balkan/balkan0.htm. (accessed July 18, 2009).

Medved, Anja and Nadja Velušček. *Mesto na travniku: videoesej o Novi Gorici.* Directed by Radovan Čok. Nova Gorica: Moja Meja, 2002. DVD.

Morpurgo, Marcello. *Valdirose: memorie della communita ebraica di Gorizia.* Udine: Del Bianco, 1986.

Novak, Bogdan C. *Trieste 1941-1954, The Ethnic, Political, and Ideological Struggle.* Chicago: University of Chicago Press, 1970.

"Oltre il confine/Čez mejo." In *Isonzo Soča, Giornale di Frontiera,* no. 57 (April-May, 2004): 11.

Pahor, Boris. *Necropolis.* Translated by Michael Biggins. Champaign: Dalkey Archive Press, 2010.

Palermo, Francesco and Giulia Predonzani. "The Slovene Minority in Italy: Unfinished Protection." October 28, 2008. *Osservatorio Balcani e Caucaso.* http://www.balcanicaucaso.org.

Patat, Luciano. *Terra di frontiera, Fascismo, guerra e dopoguerra nell' Isontino e nella Bassa friulana.* Gorizia: Centro Isontino de Ricerca e Documentazione Storica e Sociale "Leopoldo Gasparini," 2002.

Pavia, Aldo and Antonella Tiburzi. *Non perdoneró mai.* Portogruaro (Venezia): Nuova dimensione, 2006.

"Perchè la Psicoanalisi." In *Izonzo Soča, Giornale di Frontiera,* no. 6 (1991): 2-3.

"Relazione della Commissione mista storico-culturale italo-slovena: Un tentativo di costruire una memoria storica condivisa dopo un secolo di tragiche contrapposizioni." Primavera, 2001. http://www.storicamente.org/commissione_mista.pdf.

Risiera di San Sabba Monumento Nazionale. Comune di Trieste, 1995.

Schawe, Karin,ed. *KZ-Gedenkstätte Neuengamme.* Translated by Georg Felix Harsch, Hamburg: Neuengamme Concentration Camp Memorial, 2010.

"Uno Sguardo alla Storia." In *Isonzo-Soča, Giornale di Frontiera,* nos. 82-83 (2009): 6-25.

Shaine, Frederick M., trans. *And No Quarter: An Italian Partisan in World War II: Memoirs of Giovanni Pesce.* Ohio University Press, 1972.

Shephard, Ben. *After Daybreak: The Liberation of Bergen-Belsen, 1945.* New York: Schocken Books, 2005.

Sighele, Chiara. "Italian-Slovene Commission: Toward Shared History." April 22, 2008. *Osservatorio Balcani e Caucaso.* http://www.balcanicaucaso.org.

Sluga, Glenda. *The Problem of Trieste and the Italo-Yugoslav Border: Difference, Identity, and Sovereignty in Twentieth-Century Europe.* Albany: State University of New York, 2001.

Tavano, Sergio, ed. *L'Immagine di Gorizia.* Gorizia: Il Comune, 1974.

Valussi, Giorgio. *Il confine Nordorientale d'Italia.* Gorizia: Istituto di sociologia Internazionale di Gorizia, 2000.

Wald, Susanne. "'E Tornai Vivo Dall'Inferno dei Morti.' Deportati italiani nel campo di concentramento di Neuengamme." In *Il Libro dei Deportati, Volume III, La galassia concentrazionaria SS 1933-1945,* edited by Brunello Mantelli and Nicola Tranfaglia, 422-441. Milano: Mursia, 2010.

Wise, Wm. H. and Company, Inc., ed. *Pictorial History of the Second World War, Vol.1. New York, 1944.*

——. *Pictorial History of the Second World War, Vol.5,6.* New York, 1946.

Yad Vashem Photo Archives 4613/82. http://www.yadvashem. org/yv/en/exhibitions/this_month/september/09.asp. (accessed August 5, 2009).

ACKNOWLEDGEMENTS

I wish to thank all who contributed to the contents of this book. Foremost, I am grateful to my mother who had the strength to tell her story, which was sometimes painful to hear, but which I felt compelled to know. As a technical corporal in the American Blue Devil 88th Army Division stationed in Gorizia from 1946 to 1947, my father, Eugene, was able to share his experience and historical perspective of the occupying force during the precarious Italian-Yugoslav border situation after World War II.

My sister, Nadia, and brother-in-law, Dario Stasi, were instrumental in the writing of this book. They familiarized me with regional history and led me to invaluable resources. I am especially grateful to Dario, who, as Director of *Isonzo-Soča, Giornale di Frontiera,* shared his knowledge and provided me with numerous historical photos of the region. Nadia spent many hours translating text from Italian to English and took considerable time to discuss and review my work during its many stages.

The Jewish regional history and resources of the Synagogue of Gorizia were generously shared by Claudio Bulfoni. Bojana

Gulin and Marina Rossetti made themselves available when I needed text translated into Slovene or German respectively.

I wish to give special thanks to Susanne Wald, who has been an invaluable resource to me as I attempted to learn more about Neuengamme and my grandfather's fate. An employee of the Neuengamme concentration Camp Memorial, she introduced me to her research and writing on the Italian deportees at Neuengamme, recommended essential sources and reviewed my writing to ensure an accurate portrayal of that camp.

I visited the Bergen-Belsen Memorial, the solemn site of the concentration camp. The helpful and knowledgeable staff has created an ideal setting for educational encounters and research. I wish to thank Elfriede Shultz and others who have worked to compile and document information on the Bergen-Belsen prisoners and respond to inquiries from survivors or their relatives by sharing their data.

I greatly appreciate the comments of Lisa Brumberger, Suzy Camara, Robert and Susan Catherwood, Mary Ann Keck and Sue Nitschke, who were interested in reading my manuscript. Mary Beth Egeling not only made helpful comments, but provided the guidance which led me to publication. As graphic designer, Julie Eggers patiently worked with me on map design and skillfully created the book's cover from a historic regional photo, provided through the courtesy of the Musei Provinciali of Gorizia. I am grateful to my dedicated editor, Lisa Benwitz, who challenged and encouraged me to create a better book.

I thank all my friends who gave me encouragement throughout the years I worked to write this memoir. Finally, I am extremely grateful to my husband, Bill and children, Ben and Carrie, who offered me encouragement, provided technical support and patiently stood by me as I spent many years transcribing oral history, researching, and writing this book.

ABOUT THE AUTHOR

Silvia Hollenbaugh has been an advocate for tolerance in her role as teacher of English for Speakers of Other Languages for over twenty years. In this, her first book, she continues to educate on the topic of tolerance in a field of historical significance. Residing in Rochester, New York with her husband, she has two children and two grandsons. She travels to Gorizia each year to visit her mother, father and sister who have lived there for more than forty-five years.

Figure 35. Milena with her daughter Silvia, author of her memoir (2014)

Figure 36. Milena (2014)

Figure 37. Milena with husband, Eugene, a former member of the American Blue Devil 88th Army Division, which was honored by the city of Gorizia in 2007 for their contribution to the peace-keeping efforts during the post WWII years. Milena and Eugene have been married for 67 years. (2014)

CPSIA information can be obtained at www.ICGtesting.com
Printed in the USA
BVOW11s1727180915

418557BV00002B/4/P